Reading Lessons Through Literature

Level 3

Kathy Jo DeVore

www.barefootmeandering.com
veritas • gnaritas • libertas

Table of Contents

Appendices   405

Quick Start

This introduction focuses on getting you started. If you want more information about the Orton-Gillingham method of reading and spelling instruction and the importance of teaching phonograms, please see Appendix A.

Reading Lessons Through Literature has three parts. Following is an overview of each part.

Part 1. Begin teaching the phonograms. There are some slight differences between Orton programs regarding which phonograms are taught. This program teaches seventy-five basic phonograms.

Part 2. After you've taught the first 26 phonograms (*a* to *z*), begin teaching the spelling words. Simple but explicit instructions are given for having children start their own spelling notebooks. Spelling rules are referred to when applicable. Children can generally learn 10-15 words per week in Kindergarten, 20 words per week in 1st grade, and 40 words per week in 2nd grade.

Part 3. After you've taught the first 200 spelling words (lists 1-A through 1-T), you can introduce the stories. Spelling lists are arranged around the stories in the Elson Readers. The stories are divided into 173 readings which correspond to the spelling lists. A child may read a story when he's learned all the words in a story and is comfortable reading the words from his spelling notebook. It is fine if he still needs to sound the words out, but he should not be struggling.

Necessary Materials

Children learn to both read and write the phonograms in this program. This can be in the optional workbook, on a white board, in a sand tray, or any other method you wish. Instructions are included later in this introduction for adapting the program for a child who is unable to learn to write while he learns to read.

Children do need a place to write spelling words. You can either print and use the blank page from the workbook or purchase a primary composition book for this notebook. Primary composition books are produced by both Mead® and Roaring Spring. If you use the blank page from the workbook, keep the spelling lists separate from the rest of the workbook. Children should read their spelling words daily, so it's best if they don't have to search for them.

Part 1: The Phonograms

Part 1 contains a page for each of the 75 basic phonograms. It is set-up with one phonogram per page in order to make flashcards unnecessary. If you prefer flashcards, a free set is available to download on my site.

Children begin by learning the basic phonograms. Four to five year olds can learn at least two phonograms per day. Older children can often learn four per day without difficulty.

Each phonogram page has the phonogram with its sound(s) just below it. Some phonograms contain

a line that lists advanced phonogram sounds—these should be skipped for new readers; see the section "Basic and Advanced Phonograms" just before the phonogram pages. After the sounds and advanced sounds is a sample word for each sound—this is for the parent, not the child.

Children should learn to read and write two new phonograms each day. The method is simple and follows a multisensory approach. Seeing, hearing, saying, and doing—these are the basics in multisensory learning. Using multiple senses to learn new information helps the brain process the information, which helps children to remember the information better and longer.

- During the oral portion of the lesson, using either the phonogram pages in this book or flashcards, have children

Sample phonogram pages. The left is from the optional workbook. The right is an example of how to set up a phonogram page in a primary composition book.

repeat the sound(s) of each phonogram several times while looking at it.

- Before moving to the written portion of the lesson, have children practice making the phonograms in other ways while saying the sounds. Start with large motions, having them write the phonograms in the air. Move on to smaller motions by having them use a finger to trace the phonograms, either on paper or using sandpaper letters. You can also use blocks or wooden letters.

- During the written portion of the lesson, have children say the sound(s) of each phonogram while writing it approximately six to eight times. This can be in the optional workbook, in a composition book, on a white board, in a sand tray, or any other method you wish.

Learning the phonograms, or even just the basic sounds of the twenty-six letters of the alphabet, is not a simple task. Children will forget the sounds, but that's okay. Just keep moving forward and eventually the sounds will stick. Help them with the sounds when they forget. I do this quickly while reviewing. If the child hesitates, I say the sound(s); I have the child repeat the sound(s); and I move on to the next phonogram.

Do not stop teaching new phonograms. It feels counter-intuitive, but they do not have to know the phonograms perfectly before being introduced to more phonograms or beginning spelling. In fact, using the phonograms in spelling will actually help them remember the phonograms better.

A phonogram can make up to six sounds. Sample words are given to help the instructor identify each sound, but they are for the instructors, not the children. We do not want to give children extra steps to wade through, like words or pictures, while trying to remember the sounds.

An internet search will yield audio files of the phonograms being spoken. It is important to say only the phonogram sound; remember that *b* says /b/, not /buh/. Also, it is important to teach the sounds of the letters, not the names, as only the sounds are necessary for reading. The names of the letters can be taught later. Once the sounds are firmly memorized, I begin casually referring to the letters by name instead of by their phonogram names.

While teaching, the "name" of a phonogram is the sound or sounds that the phonogram makes. However, in some cases, it includes a phrase to help differentiate one phonogram from another with the exact, or almost exact, same sound(s). The phonogram name—the sound(s) plus any identifying phrase—is what children initially learn to say when they see that phonogram. For instance, the phonogram *ck* is taught as "/k/, two letter /k/." This differentiates it from *k* which makes the same single sound.

Some phonograms are taught with an applicable spelling rule. For instance, English words do not end in the letter *i*, so the phonogram *ai* is "/ā/, two letter /ā/ that we may not use at the end of English words." After a child has learned this well, he can simply say, "/ā/, two letter /ā/," during reviews. Occasionally, ask, "May it be used at the end of English words?" as part of the review.

Once the first 26 phonograms—*a* through *z*—are learned, children will begin learning spelling words, which then eases them into reading.

Part 2: The Spelling Lists

Begin dictating spelling words after teaching all of the single letter phonograms; these are *a* to *z*, so the last single letter phonogram is z.

The spelling lists are made up of some of the most common words in the English language, but they are also arranged around the stories in the Elson Readers. Level 1 includes the stories from the Elson Readers Primer; Level 2 includes the stories from the Elson Readers Book 1; Level 3 includes the stories from the Elson Readers Book 2; and Level 4 includes the stories from the Elson Readers Book 3.

1–A	
top	not
but	hat
cat	bed
red	ran
six	run

Children can generally learn 10-15 words per week in Kindergarten, 20 words per week in 1st grade, and 40 words per week in 2nd grade. Full instructions for dictating the spelling lists are in Part 2. The following is just a basic overview.

Begin dictating 10-15 spelling words per week to the child while continuing to teach two new phonograms per day. You can dictate two or three words per day, five words two or three times per week, or any combination that works for you. For children still developing fine motor control, a few words every day can help them exercise those muscles without the stress that more writing would cause.

Children will create their own spelling notebooks. They should read their spelling words daily. The spelling lists give explicit instructions for both student and instructor, but the phonogram sounds are not listed in the spelling lists. It is assumed that the instructor will learn the phonograms the same way the student will—through repetition. Until then, I recommend printing out a copy of the list of phonograms and keeping it handy during lessons. You can download phonogram posters from our site which can be printed on regular letter paper, front and back, for a handy one-page quick reference guide.

Read each word out loud. Pronounce each word carefully, exaggerating any vowel sounds that tend to be indistinct in normal speech. Give the word phonogram by phonogram as the child writes it; have the child leave a space between syllables; and then have the child read the word aloud. Phonograms are marked according to which of their sounds they make in a given word and by which spelling rules apply to them. This is explained further in Part 2.

Part 3: The Readers

Level 1 teaches 200 spelling words (lists 1-A through 1-T) before the first story. After these words have been taught, and the child is comfortable reading them—perhaps still sounding out words, but not struggling—the stories can be introduced.

Spelling lists are arranged around the stories in the Elson Readers. Each list corresponds to the story with the same number. Part 3 in this book contains the stories from one of the Elson Readers.

In the first three levels, children will not encounter a word in their reading until they have first analyzed the word, the base word, or the word with another affix as a spelling word. Children may read a story when they have learned all the words in a story and are comfortable reading the words from their spelling notebooks. Again, it's okay if children still need to sound out the words, but they should not be struggling.

The Elson Readers include traditional stories, folk tales, and fables; stories about nature and festivals; and poetry, including Mother Goose rhymes and poems by poets such as Christina G. Rossetti and Robert Louis Stevenson. Retellings of old tales have been simplified, but not dumbed down.

I have made some changes to these classic readers. Archaic animal names have been changed to reflect the more common modern names. I've made minor changes in punctuation and wording. And finally, I've removed the majority of the pictures, usually leaving only one per story. While the original artwork by L. Kate Deal is quite charming, I believe that it's best that beginning readers do not have picture clues to the text. That can encourage guessing instead of practicing decoding skills.

Part of the philosophy behind the Lessons Through Literature programs is to help children progress in incremental steps. In the Elson Readers Primer, included in Level 1, the multi-letter phonograms are underlined and multi-syllable words are written with the syllables separated, for two reasons. First, this supports the beginning reader in reading longer words while he's still learning. Second, because some rules explain when vowels say their long sounds in syllables, seeing the syllables reinforces those rules. In the Elson Readers Book 1, included in Level 2, the stories still have multi-syllable words written with the syllables separated. And finally, in the Elson Readers Book 2, included in Level 3, the stories are written in the normal fashion. In this way, children are able to gradually move from many helps in the stories to no help at all.

Daily Tasks

You can see very general sample schedules in Part 2. More specific sample schedules are in Appendix C.

While working through Part 1:

1. Review orally all the phonograms which have been learned.

2. Learn to read and write two new phonograms. During the oral portion of the lesson, have the child say the sound(s) of each phonogram while looking at it. Air write and finger trace the phonograms. During the written portion of the lesson, have the child say the sound(s) of each phonogram while writing it. This can be in the workbook, on a white board, in a sand tray, or any other method you wish.

After you've taught all of the phonograms, review the letters of the alphabet while teaching capital letters in the same way.

3. This step is not strictly necessary, but it can be helpful. Once or twice a week, have a phonogram quiz. Call out the phonograms while the child writes them. Again, use any method of writing that you wish. If necessary, give a hint on how to

start the first letter of the phonogram, or you may show the phonogram briefly.

When you begin spelling, after learning the phonogram z:

4. Every day, read all of the spelling words already learned.

5. Dictate 10-15 new spelling words per week to the child, phonogram by phonogram. Explicit instructions are given in Part 2.

When you begin reading the stories:

6. Read, and re-read, the stories. I recommend that new readers read each story at least twice. Once the child is reading more fluently, it is enough to read each story only once. If you have a child who finds reading the same story twice more frustrating than encountering new words, by all means, skip the second reading. He may, however, find a second reading more enjoyable than just reading his spelling notebook.

Although the spelling lists are arranged around the stories in the Elson Readers, they are also padded with words from the Ayres List, a list of a thousand of the most commonly used words in the English language. Not all of the spelling words will appear in the stories.

Slowing the Pace or Taking a Break

If you take a break from new lessons, it is recommended that you continue to review the phonograms and spelling words already learned. This can be done orally in a small amount of time.

Review Rather Than Spelling Tests

The only thing necessary for teaching spelling is to teach children to analyze words and then give them plenty of practice. They do this first through the spelling lists and then later through prepared dictation (explained in Appendix B). In our household, the only way we ever review the spelling words is by reading them.

I don't believe in spelling tests. Even when we do dictation, we do prepared dictation, which allows the student time to see and study the words before writing or typing them, because when we spell a word incorrectly, the wrong answer imprints on the brain just as a correct answer does. Charlotte Mason said it well in Home Education:

> Once the eye sees a misspelt word, that image remains; and if there is also the image of the word rightly spelt, we are perplexed as to which is which. Now we see why there could not be a more ingenious way of making bad spellers than 'dictation' as it is commonly taught. Every misspelt word is an image in the child's brain not to be obliterated by the right spelling. It becomes, therefore, the teacher's business to prevent false spelling, and, if an error has been made, to hide it away, as it were, so that the impression may not become fixed (242).

Every time children spell words incorrectly, it's another block towards spelling those words correctly. I've heard people make references to this particular phenomenon my entire life, and I've seen it with my own children. It is best to not see incorrectly spelled words while one is still learning. I tried a spelling program only once before discovering the O-G method. My oldest son had a proofreading exercise. At the end of it, after seeing words spelled incorrectly, he was no longer able to spell the words which he could previously spell without difficulty.

For my very visual firstborn, seeing words spelled incorrectly was enough. Consider that when a child spells a word incorrectly on a spelling test, he is using multiple senses. He is seeing the word and writing it down. In practice tests, he has likely spelled the word incorrectly out loud as well. Everything you hear about multisensory learning works in reverse as well.

The only point to a spelling test is to inform the instructor of the child's ability. Please consider that for a moment. Think carefully on this. A spelling test has absolutely no benefit to the child. For the child who is struggling with spelling, by placing those incorrectly spelled words in the child's mind, the spelling test has actually become a stumbling block to correct spelling. But even the child who has no trouble with spelling has not benefitted from the exercise.

Young children who are fairly new readers are still internalizing spelling, from their reading and also from explicit spelling instruction. I leave this process alone to work slowly in the background. I do not test to see if it's working.

In our household, here's how this plays out: I don't put my children in a position to fail while they're still going through this process. That means that I do not require original written work from my children in the early grades. They do copywork. They do oral narrations, which I write for them. I don't prevent them from doing their own writing, but I never require it. By the time I begin requiring writing from them, when they begin doing their own written narrations and prepared dictations around 3rd or 4th grade, they're ready for them.

For those who really feel the need to do more with the spelling lists with younger children, you can use our optional copywork book which includes the entire text of the Elson Readers Primer. This is the path that I recommend.

Non-Writers

Some children have problems which prevent them from learning to write, but they are ready to learn to read. My older three boys all learned to read without a writing component to their lessons. So, while I do believe the writing helps, I also recognize that it's not strictly necessary to learn to read. I hope these instructions will help you adapt the program if you have a child who cannot do the writing portion.

When you introduce the phonograms, simply skip the writing portion of the lesson. If possible, work on letter formation through air writing or finger tracing the letters.

When it is time to begin the spelling lists, use phonogram flashcards or tiles; both are available as free downloads from our website. It's important to use something with phonograms, not letters, because we want children thinking in terms of phonograms rather than individual letters. Make sure that you have enough cards or tiles to complete each word in the list. As you dictate each word (explained more fully in Part 2), have children identify each phonogram as you call it out and put the phonograms together to form the word. Then, write the word in the spelling book and have the child mark it as much as possible. Alternatively, explain the markings as you make them. Later, have the child tell you how to mark the words.

Using Reading Lessons as a Spelling Program

Once children have begun to read fluently, you can focus on using Reading Lessons Through Literature as a spelling program rather than a reading instruction program.

While children are learning to read, instructors might dictate as many as 40-50 words per week, depending on the ages of the children. However, as a spelling program, you can slow the pace down to 10-20 words per week and spend more time on reading. A good goal after attaining reading fluency is to complete one level of Reading Lessons per school year. Using Reading Lessons in this way provides a prolonged period of study and practice with the phonograms and spelling rules. This will continue to reinforce what the child has already learned while keeping his skills sharp until he is old enough to begin prepared dictation.

If you are beginning Reading Lessons as a spelling program with an older, fluent reader, I recommend going through Level 1 at a quick pace before slowing down to one level per school year.

Because Reading Lessons is based on practice and repetition, I do recommend that everyone starts in Level 1. The student may already know how to spell all of the words, but if he's new to analyzing words, it will be helpful to begin with the easiest words. The exception is for people who have some experience with an O-G program which utilizes phonograms and marks spelling words. If you have this experience and are strongly opposed to starting at Level 1, I recommend Level 2. It is important to note that children learn all 75 phonograms in Level 1, so the lists in Level 2 assume that the student already knows all the phonograms.

Struggling Spellers

For older students who struggle with spelling, a more intense course of study may be necessary. The spelling lists in Reading Lessons include the complete Ayres List—1,000 of the most common words in English as compiled by Leonard Ayres in the early 1900s—in addition to the 1,500 other words necessary to read the stories. Mastering these words will give students a good foundation.

To accomplish this, you can go through the books at a faster pace, multiple times. For instance, dictate 30-50 words per week. Complete Levels 1 and 2 at this pace, then start over with Level 2. Complete Levels 2 and 3, then start over with Level 3. Continue until you have gone through each book twice.

In addition to the spelling words, use the readers—once these words have been analyzed by the student—for copywork. You can also add prepared copywork: Choose a copywork passage and have the student analyze several words from the passage before copying it. When the student is ready, begin prepared dictation (explained in Appendix B).

Stay the Course

A new homeschooling mother asked, "Which reading program will teach my child to read?" An experienced homeschooling mother replied, "The third one."

Sometimes, we change curricula because we read new research or we learn new information, so we change to a program that is better or better fits our own educational philosophy. But other times, we simply don't give a program time to work. Learning to read takes time, and it also relies on the developmental readiness of the child. If the methodology behind a program is sound, then there is no reason to switch programs. Reading is hard work and requires lots of practice. Whatever program you use, give it time to work.

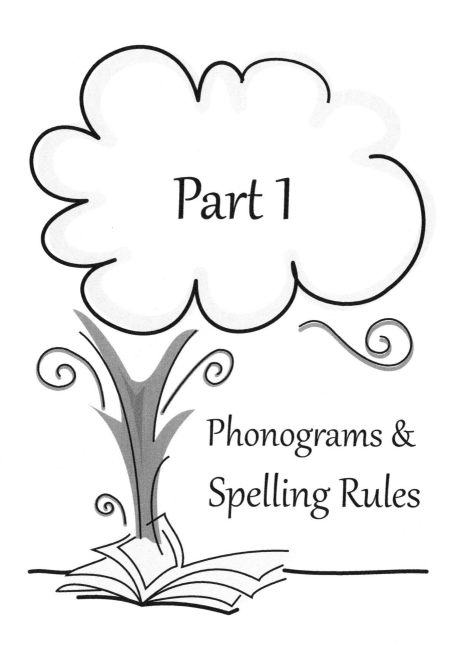

Part 1

Phonograms &
Spelling Rules

Basic and Advanced Phonograms

Advanced phonograms are ones which are uncommon or which appear in more advanced words. In addition to the advanced phonograms, some of the basic phonograms have advanced sounds.

I recommend teaching only the basic sounds of the basic phonograms to new readers to simplify matters for them. Older students may learn the advanced sounds of the basic phonograms as well as the advanced phonograms, **but keep in mind that many words with advanced phonograms can also be explained with silent letters or as exceptions.** You may never feel the need to teach the advanced phonograms at all.

The phonogram pages for the basic phonograms show both basic and advanced phonogram sounds when applicable, formatted

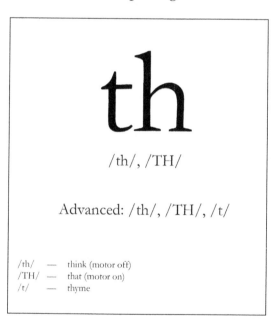

as in the sample. The advanced phonograms appear after the 75 basic phonograms; each of these pages has "Advanced Phonogram" at the top of the page. I have included them here both for the convenience of those who choose to teach them and also to make these pages a good reference guide for all stages of learning.

Some of the basic phonograms have advanced sounds. In the 75 Basic Phonograms list, only the basic sounds are listed, but the phonograms with advanced sounds have an asterisk (*) next to them. In the Advanced Phonograms list, the phonograms are listed with all of their sounds, basic and advanced, and the phonograms with basic sounds have an asterisk (*) next to them.

75 Basic Phonograms

a	/ă/, /ā/, /ä/	at, acorn, wasp
b	/b/	but
c	/k/, /s/	cat, city
d	/d/	dog
e	/ĕ/, /ē/	best, me
f	/f/	four
g	/g/, /j/	garden, gem
h	/h/	hat
i	/ĭ/, /ī/, /ē/, /y/	igloo, ice, radio, onion
j	/j/	jam
k	/k/	kite
l	/l/	lot
m	/m/	mat
n	/n/	no
o	/ŏ/, /ō/, /oo/	pot, go, to
p	/p/	put
qu	/kw/	queen
r	/r/	run
s	/s/, /z/	sass, has
t	/t/	tap
u	/ŭ/, /ū/, /ü/	umbrella, unit, put
v	/v/	vowel
w	/w/	water
x	/ks/	fox
y	/y/, /ĭ/, /ī/, /ē/	yellow, gym, sky, baby
z *	/z/	zoo
ai *	/ā/ — 2 letter /ā/ we may NOT use at the end of English words	hail
ar	/är/	car
au *	/ä/ — 2 letter /ä/ that we may NOT use at the end of English words	pauper
augh	/ä/, /af/	caught, laugh
aw	/ä/ — 2 letter /ä/ that we MAY use at the end of English words	paw
ay *	/ā/ — 2 letter /ā/ that we MAY use at the end of English words	play
bu	/b/ — 2 letter /b/	build
ch	/ch/, /k/, /sh/	church, Christ, chef
cei	/sē/	receive

ci	/sh/ — short /sh/ ("short" because it begins with a short letter)	.... facial
ck	/k/ — 2 letter /k/ .... back
dge	/j/ — 3 letter /j/ ....dodge
ea	/ē/, /ĕ/, /ā/ .... beat, dread, break
ear	/er/ as in pearl...pearl
ed	/ed/, /d/, /t/..waded, slammed, picked
ee	/ē/ — double /ē/.. tee
ei *	/ā/, /ē/, /ī/ ....their, protein, feisty
eigh	/ā/, /ī/ ....eight, height
er	/er/ as in her...her
ew	/oo/, /ū/ .... dew, few
ey *	/ā/, /ē/.. they, key
gn	/n/ — 2 letter /n/ that we use at the beginning or the end of a word
		.... gnome, sign
gu	/g/, /gw/ ....guest, language
ie	/ē/ — 2 letter /ē/ ....thief
igh	/ī/ — 3 letter /ī/ .... sight
ir	/er/ as in dirt.. dirt
kn	/n/ — 2 letter /n/ that we use only at the beginning of a base word
		....know
mb	/m/ — 2 letter /m/ .... comb
ng	/ng/.. ding (nasal sound)
oa	/ō/ — 2 letter /ō/ ....boat
oe *	/ō/, /oo/ ....doe, shoe
oi	/oi/ that we may NOT use at the end of English words ....toil
oo	/oo/, /ü/, /ō/ ....food, hook, floor
or	/or/.. cord
ou	/ow/, /ō/, /oo/, /ŭ/, /ü/ .... our, four, tour, famous, could
ough	/ŏ/, /ō/, /oo/, /ow/, /uff/, /off/
		.... bought, dough, through, bough, rough, cough
ow	/ow/, /ō/...plow, bow
oy	/oi/ that we MAY use at the end of English words........................ toy
ph	/f/ — 2 letter /f/ ....phonics
sh	/sh/..shell
si	/sh/, /zh/ .... transgression, vision
tch	/ch/...clutch
th *	/th/, /TH/ .... think, that
ti	/sh/ — tall /sh/ ("tall" because it begins with a tall letter)....... nation
ui	/oo/...fruit
ur	/er/ as in turn... turn
wh	/wh/.. wheel
wor	/wer/..worm
wr	/r/ — 2 letter /r/ ....wreck

Advanced Phonograms

ae	/ā/, /ē/, /ĕ/	aerial, algae, aesthetic
ah	/ä/	blah
ai *	/ā/, /ī/, /ă/	mail, aisle, plaid
au *	/ä/, /ō/, /ā/, /ow/	pauper, chauffeur, gauge, sauerkraut
ay *	/ā/, /ī/	day, cayenne
cc	/ch/	cappuccino
ce	/sh/	ocean
cu	/k/, /kw/	biscuit, cuisine
eau	/ō/, /ū/, /ŏ/	bureau, beauty, bureaucracy
ei *	/ā/, /ē/, /ī/, /ĭ/, /ĕ/	their, protein, feisty, forfeit, heifer
et	/ā/	ballet
eu	/oo/, /ū/	neutral, feud
ey *	/ā/, /ē/, /ī/	they, turkey, geyser
ge	/j/, /zh/	surgeon, mirage
gh	/g/	ghost
oe *	/ō/, /oo/, /ē/	toe, shoe, subpoena
ot	/ō/	depot
our	/er/	journey
pn	/n/	pneumonia
ps	/s/	psalm
pt	/t/	pterodactyl
rh	/r/	rhyme
sc	/s/	science
sci	/ch/	conscience
th *	/th/, /TH/, /t/	thought, them, thyme
ut	/ū/	debut
yr	/ēr/, /er/	lyric, syrup
z *	/z/, /s/	zoo, quartz

30 Spelling Rules

Vowel and Vowel Sound Rules
1. **Q** always needs **u**, and **u** is not a vowel here.
2. **C** says /s/ before **e**, **i**, and **y**. Otherwise, **c** says /k/: picnic, picnicking.
3. **G** may say /j/ before **e**, **i**, and **y**. Otherwise, **g** says /g/.
4. Vowels **a, e, o, u** usually say /ā, ē, ō, ū/ at the end of a syllable.
5. Vowels **y** and **i** may say /ĭ/, /ī/, or /ē/ at the end of a syllable.
6. Vowel **y** says /ī/ at the end of a one-syllable word: by, sky, why.
7. Vowel **y** says /ē/ only at the end of a multi-syllable word: baby, candy.
8. Vowels **i** and **o** may say /ī/ and /ō/ when followed by two consonants.
9. At the end of a base word, /ā/ is usually spelled **ay**. There are ten exceptions when /ā/ is spelled **ey**: convey, hey, ley, obey, osprey, prey, purvey, survey, they, whey.
10. At the end of words, vowel **a** says its third sound: ma, zebra.
11. The **gh** phonograms **augh**, **ough**, **igh**, and **eigh** can each be used only at the end of a base word or before the letter **t**. The **gh** is either silent or it says /f/.

End of Base Word Rules
12. Engish words do not end in **i, u, v,** or **j**, but YOU and I are special.
13. Phonograms **dge** and **ck** are used only after a single vowel which says its short sound.
14. Phonogram **tch** is used only after a single vowel which does not say its long sound.
    Phonogram **tch** is the phonogram usually used to say /ch/ following a single vowel at the end of base words, but **ch** says /ch/ after a single vowel at the end of six base words: attach, spinach, rich, which, much, such. Phonogram **ch** is used at the end of base words following two vowels (teach, preach) and after a vowel followed by a consonant (church, bunch).
15. We often double **f, l,** and **s** after a single vowel at the end of a base word. We sometimes double other letters.

5 Reasons for Final Silent E

16. (1) The vowel says its name because of the *e*.
17. (2) English words do not end in *v* or *u*.
18. (3) The *e* makes *c* say /s/ or *g* say /j/.
19. (4) Every syllable must have a written vowel.
20. (5) Miscellaneous silent *e* covers all other silent *e* usages. This can include preventing a word that would otherwise end in *s* from looking plural, making a word appear larger, making *th* say /TH/, and making homonyms appear different.

Affix Rules

21. When added to another syllable, the prefix all- and the suffix -full each drop an *l*: almost, truthful.
22. When adding a vowel suffix, drop the final silent *e* unless it is still necessary according to other spelling rules, such as making *c* say /s/ or *g* say /j/: charge, chargeable, charging.
23. When adding a vowel suffix to a word ending in one vowel followed by one consonant, double the last letter only if the word is one syllable or the last syllable is accented: begin, beginning; worship, worshiping. Do not double *x*, *w*, or *y*.
24. The single vowel *y* (not part of a multi-letter phonogram) changes to *i* before adding any ending unless the ending begins with *i*: happy, happiness; try, tries, trying. This is because...
25. English words cannot have two letters *i* in a row.
26. To form the past tense of regular verbs, add *ed*. *Ed* forms a new syllable when the base word ends in the sound /d/ or /t/. Otherwise, *ed* says /d/ or /t/.
27. Use *s* to make regular nouns plural and to make the third person singular form of a regular verb. Use *es* after phonograms that hiss: *s*, *ch*, *sh*, *x*, and *z*. Refer to rule 23 when adding *es*. *Ch* does not hiss when it says /k/: stomach, stomachs.

Spelling Sh Rules

28. *Sh* spells /sh/ at the begininning of words and at the end of syllables. It never spells /sh/ at the beginning of any syllable after the first one except for the ending —ship: she, fish, hardship.
29. *Ti*, *si*, and *ci* say /sh/ at the beginning of any syllable except the first one. Look to the root word to determine which one to use: par*t*, par*ti*al; transgres*s*, transgres*si*on; fa*c*e, fa*ci*al.

Miscellaneous Rule

30. *Z* says /z/ at the beginning of a base word, never *s*.

C

/k/, /s/

/k/ — cat
/s/ — city

a

/ă/, /ā/, /ä/

/ă/   —   at

/ā/   —   acorn

/ä/   —   wasp

d

/d/

/d/ — dog

g

/g/, /j/

/g/ — garden
/j/ — gem

O

/ŏ/, /ō/, /oo/

/ŏ/ — pot
/ō/ — go
/oo/ — to

qu

/kw/, /k/

/kw/ — queen
/k/ — croquet

i

/ĭ/, /ī/, /ē/, /y/

/ĭ/   —   igloo
/ī/   —   ice
/ē/   —   radio
/y/   —   onion

These sounds are the same as those of **y**, only the order is different. To improve memory retention, chant:

/ĭ/, /ī/, /ē/   [pause]   /y/

j

/j/

/j/ — jam

/m/

/m/ — mat

/n/

/n/ — no

/r/

/r/   —   run

l

/l/

/l/   —   lot

h

/h/

/h/ — hat

k

/k/

/k/ — kite

b

/b/

/b/ — but

p

/p/

/p/ — put

t

/t/

/t/ — tap

u

/ŭ/, /ū/, /ü/

/ŭ/ — umbrella
/ū/ — unit
/ü/ — put

/y/, /ĭ/, /ī/, /ē/

/y/	—	yellow
/ĭ/	—	gym
/ī/	—	sky
/ē/	—	baby

These sounds are the same as those of *i*, only the order is different. To improve memory retention, chant:

/y/   [pause]   /ĭ/, /ī/, /ē/

e

/ĕ/, /ē/

/ĕ/ — best
/ē/ — me

/f/

/f/ — four

S

/s/, /z/

/s/ — sass
/z/ — has

[Note: The second sound for *s* is /z/. However, the sounds are so similar that students will automatically adjust to the correct pronunciation for the word that they are reading, so it is possible to just teach the first sound.}

V

/v/

/v/ — vowel

W

/w/

/w/ — water

X

/ks/, /z/

/ks/ — fox
/z/ — xylophone

Z

/z/

Advanced: /z/, /s/

/z/ — zoo
/s/ — quartz

[Note: The advanced sound of **z** is /s/. However, the sounds are so similar that students will automatically adjust to the correct pronunciation for the word that they are reading, so it is possible to just teach the basic sound.]

Begin Part 2.

/th/, /TH/

Advanced: /th/, /TH/, /t/

/th/ — think (motor off)
/TH/ — that (motor on)
/t/ — thyme

[Note: The second sound of **th** is /TH/. However, the sounds
are so similar that students will automatically adjust to the correct
pronunciation for the word that they are reading, so it is possible to
just teach the first sound.]

ck

/k/ — 2 letter /k/

/k/   —   back

ai

/ā/ — 2 letter /ā/ that we may NOT use at the end of English words

Advanced: /ā/, /ī/, /ă/

/ā/	—	hail
/ī/	—	aisle
/ă/	—	plaid

ay

/ā/ — 2 letter /ā/ that we MAY
use at the end of English words

Advanced: /ā/, /ī/

/ā/ — play
/ī/ — cayenne

sh

/sh/

/sh/ — shell

ng

/ng/

/ng/ — ding (nasal sound)

ee

/ē/ — double /ē/

/ē/   —   tee

/oo/, /ü/, /ō/

/oo/	—	food
/ü/	—	hook
/ō/	—	floor

ou

/ow/, /ō/, /oo/, /ŭ/, /ü/

/ow/	—	our
/ō/	—	four
/oo/	—	tour
/ŭ/	—	famous
/ü/	—	could, should, would

[Note: Although the /ü/ sound occurs only in the above three base words, it is included in order to avoid making these common base words exceptions.]

OW

/ow/, /ō/

/ow/ — plow
/ō/ — bow

ar

/är/

/är/ — car

ch

/ch/, /k/, /sh/

/ch/ — church
/k/ — chasm
/sh/ — chef

au

/ä/ — 2 letter /ä/ that we may NOT
use at the end of English words

Advanced: /ä/, /ō/, /ā/, /ow/

/ä/	—	pauper
/ō/	—	chauffeur
/ā/	—	gauge
/ow/	—	sauerkraut

aw

/ä/ — 2 letter /ä/ that we MAY
use at the end of English words

/ä/   —   paw

oi

/oi/ that we may NOT use at
the end of English words

/oi/   —   toil

oy

/oi/ that we MAY use at the
end of English words

/oi/ — toy

er

/er/ as in h<u>er</u>

/er/ — her

The four spellings of /er/: Oyst<u>er</u>s t<u>ur</u>n d<u>ir</u>t into p<u>ear</u>ls.

M<u>er</u>maids t<u>ur</u>n and tw<u>ir</u>l with p<u>ear</u>ls.

ur

/er/ as in t<u>ur</u>n

/ur/ — turn

The four spellings of /er/: Oyst<u>er</u>s t<u>ur</u>n d<u>ir</u>t into p<u>ear</u>ls.

M<u>er</u>maids t<u>ur</u>n and tw<u>ir</u>l with p<u>ear</u>ls.

ir

/er/ as in d<u>ir</u>t

/er/ — dirt

The four spellings of /er/: Oyst<u>er</u>s t<u>ur</u>n d<u>ir</u>t into p<u>ear</u>ls.

M<u>er</u>maids t<u>ur</u>n and tw<u>ir</u>l with p<u>ear</u>ls.

ear

/er/ as in p<u>ear</u>l

/er/ — pearl

The four spellings of /er/: Oyst<u>er</u>s t<u>ur</u>n d<u>ir</u>t into p<u>ear</u>ls.

M<u>er</u>maids t<u>ur</u>n and tw<u>ir</u>l with p<u>ear</u>ls.

wor

/wer/

/wer/ — worm

/wh/

/wh/ — wheel

ea

/ē/, /ĕ/, /ā/

/ē/	—	beat
/ĕ/	—	bread
/ā/	—	break

or

/or/

/or/ — cord

ed

/ed/, /d/, /t/

/ed/ — waded
/d/ — washed
/t/ — picked

[Note: **Ed** is the ending used to form the past tense of regular verbs. **Ed** forms a new syllable when the base word ends in **d** or **t**. Otherwise, **ed** says /d/ or /t/.]

ew

/oo/, /ū/

/oo/ — dew
/ū/ — few

cei

/sē/

/sē/ — receive

gu

/g/, /gw/

/g/ — guest
/gw/ — language

wr

/r/ — 2 letter /r/

/r/   —   wreck

augh

/ä/, /ăf/

/ä/ — caught
/ăf/ — laugh

ui

/oo/

/oo/ — fruit

oa

/ō/ — 2 letter /ō/

/ō/   —   boat

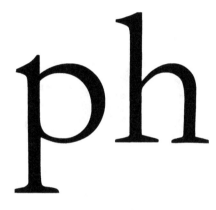

ph

/f/ — 2 letter /f/

/f/ — phonics

oe

/ō/, /oo/

Advanced: /ō/, /oo/, /ē/

/ō/   —   doe
/oo/   —   shoe
/ē/   —   subpoena

tch

/ch/

/ch/ — clutch

dge

/j/ — 3 letter /j/

/j/   —   dodge

ey

/ā/, /ē/

Advanced: /ā/, /ē/, /ī/

/ā/	—	they
/ē/	—	key
/ī/	—	geyser

bu

/b/ — 2 letter /b/

/bu/ — build

ei

/ā/, /ē/, /ī/

Advanced: /ā/, /ē/, /ī/, /ĭ/, /ĕ/

/ā/	—	their
/ē/	—	protein
/ī/	—	feisty
/ĭ/	—	forfeit
/ĕ/	—	heifer

eigh

/ā/, /ī/

/ā/	—	eight
/ī/	—	height

ci

/sh/ — short /sh/

"short" because it begins with a short letter

/sh/ — facial

ti

/sh/ — tall /sh/

"tall" because it begins with a tall letter

/sh/ — nation

si

/sh/, /zh/

/sh/ — transgression
/zh/ — vision

kn

/n/ — 2 letter /n/ that we use only at
the beginning of a base word

/n/   —   know

igh

/ī/ — 3 letter /ī/

/ī/   —   sight

ie

/ē/ — 2 letter /ē/

/ē/   —   thief

gn

/n/ — 2 letter /n/ that we can use at
the beginning or the end of a word

/gn/ — gnarl, sign

ough

/ŏ/, /ō/, /oo/,
/ow/, /ŭff/, /ŏff/

/ŏ/	—	bought
/ō/	—	dough
/oo/	—	through
/ow/	—	bough
/ŭff/	—	rough
/ŏff/	—	cough

mb

/m/ — 2 letter /m/

/m/ — comb

Advanced Phonogram

ae

/ā/, /ē/, /ĕ/

/ā/	—	aerial
/ē/	—	algae
/ĕ/	—	aesthetic

Advanced Phonogram

ah

/ä/

/ä/ — blah

Advanced Phonogram

cc

/ch/

/ch/ — cappuccino

Advanced Phonogram

ce

/sh/

/sh/ — ocean

Advanced Phonogram

cu

/k/, /kw/

/k/ — biscuit
/kw/ — cuisine

Advanced Phonogram

eau

/ō/, /ū/, /ŏ/

/ō/ — bureau
/ū/ — beauty
/ŏ/ — bureaucracy

et

/ā/

/ā/ — ballet

Advanced Phonogram

/oo/, /ū/

/oo/ — neutral
/ū/ — feud

/j/, /zh/

/j/ — surgeon
/zh/ — mirage

Advanced Phonogram

/g/

/g/   —   ghost

ot

/ō/

/ō/ — depot

Advanced Phonogram

our

/er/

/er/ — journey

Advanced sentences for the five spellings of /er/:

Oysters turn dirt into pearls courageously.

Mermaids turn and twirl on an earthly journey.

Advanced Phonogram

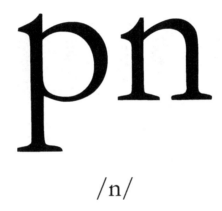

/n/

/n/ — pneumonia

Advanced Phonogram

/s/

/s/ — psalm

Advanced Phonogram

/t/

/t/ — pterodactyl

Advanced Phonogram

/r/

/r/ — rhyme

Advanced Phonogram

SC

/s/

/s/ — science

Advanced Phonogram

sci

/ch/

/ch/   —   conscience

/ū/

/ū/ — debut

Advanced Phonogram

yr

/ēr/, /er/

/ēr/, /er/ — lyric, syrup

Part 2

Spelling Lists

The Spelling Lists

The spelling lists are made up of some of the most common words in the English language, and they are arranged around the stories in The Elson Readers.

The child will be creating his own spelling notebook. You can either print and use the blank page from the optional workbook or purchase a primary composition book. Primary composition books are produced by both Mead® and Roaring Spring. The following pages give an overview of making the spelling notebook, and the spelling lists give explicit instructions for both student and instructor. Each word is read aloud, then given to the child phonogram by phonogram until he has completed the word. He then reads the word aloud. Phonograms are marked according to which of their sounds they make in a given word and by which spelling rules apply to them.

With five year old, Kindergarten age children, dictate 10-15 new words each week while continuing to teach two new phonograms per day. This can be five words two or three times per week, but if the child has trouble writing five words per day, dictate two to three new words every day.

With six to seven year old, first grade age children, dictate 20 new words to the child each week. This can be five words, four days per week, or it could be ten words twice a week.

Seven to eight year old, second grade children, can handle 40 to 50 words per week, ten words four or five days a week.

If you take a break, continue reviewing the phonograms and spelling words already covered.

In addition to the phonograms, there are also 30 spelling rules. The spelling rules are mentioned when applicable to a spelling word.

The next two pages give sample schedules and sample spelling notebook pages.

Monday	Tuesday	Wednesday	Thursday	Friday
Review Phonograms	Review Phonograms	Phonogram Quiz	Review Phonograms	Phonogram Quiz
Learn 2 New Phonograms	Learn 2 New Phonograms	Learn 2 New Phonograms	Learn 2 New Phonograms	Learn 2 New Phonograms
Read Spelling Words	Read Spelling Words	Read Spelling Words	Read Spelling Words	Read Spelling Words
Dictate 2-3 New Spelling Words	Dictate 2-3 New Spelling Words	Dictate 2-3 New Spelling Words	Dictate 2-3 New Spelling Words	Dictate 2-3 New Spelling Words

Monday	Tuesday	Wednesday	Thursday	Friday
Review Phonograms	Review Phonograms	Phonogram Quiz	Review Phonograms	Phonogram Quiz
Learn 2 New Phonograms	Learn 2 New Phonograms	Learn 2 New Phonograms	Learn 2 New Phonograms	Learn 2 New Phonograms
Read Spelling Words	Read Spelling Words	Read Spelling Words	Read Spelling Words	Read Spelling Words
Dictate 5 New Spelling Words		Dictate 5 New Spelling Words		(Optional) Dictate 5 New Spelling Words

1-A	1-B
top	and
but	all[3]
cat	tall[3]
red	am
six	be
not	a
hat	an
bed	the[2]
ran	is[2]
run	has[2]

1-A

top   not
but   hat
cat   bed
red   ran
six   run

Analyzing the Spelling Words

We use markings to analyze the spelling words. All of these markings are shown and explained next to the spelling words in the lists. You do not have to know and understand all of the markings in advance. Following are some of the most common markings used. The first two have a note included in the first twenty reading lists; after that, the word is simply marked. Notes in brackets [ ] are for the instructor, not the child.

Numbers 6 through 9 are based on spelling rules, so their markings are a bit different than the ones mentioned in 1 through 5. Since the words are marked and explained for you in the spelling lists, these are merely explanations for the markings you will see rather than a list that you need to memorize.

1. Leave a space between syllables.

fish er

2. When a phonogram does not say its first sound, put a small number above it to show which sound it makes.

3
all

3. Underline multi-letter phonograms.

fi<u>sh</u>

4. Double underline silent letters. The most common is the final silent *e* at the end of words. Final silent *e* has different functions, and these functions are often marked and discussed with the word. For instance, reason 1 silent *e* makes a vowel say its name, so a bridge is drawn from the silent *e* to the vowel instead of a number 2 over the vowel.

mine

The other reasons for silent *e* are marked with a number beside the double underline and discussed with the word. All the reasons for a final silent *e* are listed in the 30 Spelling Rules at the beginning of this book. Reason 5 is a miscellaneous silent *e*, but the others have specific reasons.

<u><u>are</u></u>$_{=5}$ Double underline the silent *e*.

5. Mark eXceptions, phonograms which don't say any of their normal sounds, with an X.

X
of

6. Underline *c* and *g* when they say /s/ and /j/ when followed by *e*, *i*, or *y*. This is a spelling rule, so the consonant receives an underline instead of a number 2 over it.

<u>c</u>ir cle   <u>g</u>erm

7. Underline *a*, *e*, *i*, *o*, and *u* when they say /ā/, /ē/, /ī/, /ō/, and /ū/ at the end of a syllable. This is a spelling rule, so the vowel receives an underline instead of a number 2 over it.

m<u>e</u>

8. Underline *i* and *o* when they say /ī/ and /ō/ when followed by two consonants. This is a spelling rule, so the vowel receives an underline instead of a number 2 over it.

c<u>o</u>lt

9. Underline *y* when it says /ī/ at the end of a one-syllable word or /ē/ at the end of a multi-syllable word. These are spelling rules, so the vowel receives an underline instead of a number over it.

sk<u>y</u>   can d<u>y</u>

Dictating the Spelling Words

1. Say the word, then say the word in a sentence if necessary or desired. I only make up a sentence when my child doesn't understand the word or when the word is a homonym.

2. Call the word out phonogram by phonogram. Give the child time to write each phonogram. Correct as necessary. If the child can't remember a phonogram, give a reminder. A white board is handy for this, but you could also use a flashcard, the phonogram pages at the front of this book, or just a sheet of paper.

For example:

top	Top. The first phonogram is /t/. The next phonogram is /ŏ/, /ō/, /oo/. The last phonogram is /p/. /t/-/ŏ/-/p/. Top.
3 all	The first phonogram is /ă/, /ā/, /ä/. Write a small 3 above it to show that it says its third sound. The next phonogram is /l/. The last phonogram is /l/. We often double /l/ after a single vowel at the end of a base word. /ä/-/l/-/l/. All.
be	The first phonogram is /b/. The next phonogram is /ĕ/, /ē/. Underline /ē/; *e* says /ē/ at the end of a syllable.

3. Have the child read the word.

Follow this format every time. After the first few words, only the additional information, such as the markings and references to spelling rules, are included.

It's important to note that this program is built upon repetition and practice. Applicable spelling rules are given with the spelling words. Over time, instructor and student will both learn these rules just from hearing and saying them so often during spelling dictation.

As you both become more comfortable with the procedure, it is also a good practice to ask the child questions to get him analyzing the words. For example:

Instructor: Is *a* making its first, second, or third sound?

Student: Second.

Instructor: It's making its second sound, so write a small 2 above it.

Instructor: Why do we need the silent *e*?

Student: Silent *e* makes *i* say /ī/.

Instructor: Double underline the silent *e*, then draw a bridge between the silent *e* and *i*.

Reading the Spelling Words

Children should read their spelling words frequently. That means daily at first. Once children have 200 words—lists 1-A through 1-T— they can begin reading the stories. At that point, you might alternate. Twice a week, children can read the new story, and on the other days, they can read their spelling words.

Once the list reaches 250 to 300 words, the list can be split into parts. For instance, have the child read the most recent 100 words, and then review 50-100 older words. We separate the spelling book with Post-it® Tabs for the sake of simplicity.

The important part is to have the child continue practicing by reading the spelling book daily. The number of words may differ between children depending on age and ability.

Sounding Out and Lazy Vowels

Some words are exceptions. This means that one of its phonograms does not make any of its normal sounds. We (sometimes) mark these phonograms with an X, but that does not help children remember the sound. I have had my children sound them out as if the word was regular. This gives them an audio clue.

As an example, let's look at the word one. When children learn one on the spelling list, we tell them, "Think to spell /ōn/." Later, when they come across it on the spelling list, we might say, "This phonogram is an exception, but sound it out as if silent *e* were making *o* say /ō/, /ō-n/. That's how the word used to be pronounced, but now we say /won/."

We can also teach that these exception words have two names, their real names and a nickname. We sound out the real name, but we call them by their nicknames.

In the first 127 spelling lists, there are 1,720 words and less than ten exceptions. I actively avoid marking exceptions because it seems that children have an easier time remembering the "nickname" after sounding the word out according to the rules rather than trying to remember what can easily become a sight word with no clues at all.

We do something similar with vowels. In English, the schwa /ə/ is the most common vowel sound. This is the common sound of a vowel in an unstressed syllable, pronounced similar to a short *u* sound—/ŭ/.

Since this information is a bit over the head of the average five year old, we can explain it by describing these vowels as lazy. The word alone is listed in the spelling list like this:

a lone   Underline /ā/ to show that it's saying /ā/ at the end of a syllable. **O** says /ō/ because of the silent **e**. Double underline the silent **e**, and draw a bridge between the **o** and the **e**.

When we sound out the word, or "think to spell," we stress the /ā/ sound, but we can point out that it is a lazy vowel, so the child will hear people say /ə-lōn/.

It is important to stress all vowel sounds in the spelling lessons. Otherwise, depending on your accent, pen and pin might be indistinguishable.

Also, remember that analyzing words is merely a tool to help us understand spelling. Some words have multiple ways to analyze them. If you see a way to analyze a word that makes more sense to you and your child, use it.

Before We Begin...

There are two kinds of letters, vowels and consonants. The vowels are *a*, *e*, *i*, *o*, and *u*. *Y* is a vowel when it is saying /ĭ/, /ī/, /ē/. When *y* says /y/, it is a consonant. All other letters are also consonants.

Vowels sounds are made when the mouth is open and the sound is not blocked by your tongue, teeth, or lips. Consonant sounds are made when the tongue, teeth, or lips do block the sound.

A syllable is a chunk of a word, and a syllable always has a vowel sound. In fact, when you count the syllables in a word, you are counting how many vowel sounds it has. That's why you can find out how many syllables a word has by seeing how many times your jaw goes down when saying the word—your jaw goes down when you open your mouth to make a vowel sound.

Affixes

Sometimes, we add to a word to make it mean something a little different. It's called a prefix if we add to the beginning of the word, and it's called a suffix if we add to the end of the word. The word without affixes is called the base word.

For instance, someone has a letter. She can **open** it if she wants, or she can leave it **unopened**. She decides she wants to see what the letter says, so now she is **opening** it. The base word is **open**, but we add prefixes and suffixes to make the word mean different things. Yesterday she **opened** it with a letter **opener**, and today she **reopens** it.

When a suffix starts with a vowel, we call it a vowel suffix.

Remember, the base word is the word without prefixes and suffixes. Sometimes the spelling of the base word changes when we add affixes, and some of these changes will be mentioned as you get your new spelling words.

One of the most common suffixes you will encounter is *ed*. You should recognize this as one of your phonograms! When we add it to the end of a word, *ed* tells us that something happened in the past. Sometimes, *ed* will just add a /d/ or /t/ sound to the end of a word. But when the base word ends in the sound /d/ or /t/, *ed* creates a new syllable. In the stories, you will see *ed* added to words you've already learned.

Homographs

Some words in your spelling lists are homographs. The prefix **homo** is from the Greek language. It means the same. **Graph** means **drawn** or **written**. So **homograph** means **same writing**. You can remember this by thinking of photographs—photographs are light drawings. Homographs look the same, but they do not mean the same thing. Since homographs are spelled the same, we can only tell which word a homograph is by looking at the context—the other words in the sentence.

Advanced Phonograms

In the following spelling lists, there is an advanced phonogram.

our   /er/ . . . . journey

Since it is a new /er/, you can add it to the ways to spell /er/ sentences: Oyst<u>er</u>s t<u>ur</u>n d<u>ir</u>t into p<u>ear</u>ls co<u>ur</u>ageously; or: M<u>er</u>maids t<u>ur</u>n and tw<u>ir</u>l on an <u>ear</u>thly jo<u>ur</u>ney.

2
re**ad** y — Underline **y**. Vowel **y** says /ē/ at the end of a multi-syllable word.

scra**tch** ing — Phonogram **tch** is used only after a single vowel which does not say its name.

l**ai**d

b**athe** — **A** says /ā/ because of the silent **e**; underline the silent **e** twice, and draw a bridge between the silent **e** and the **a**.

2   3
dress**ed** — We often double /s/ after a single vowel at the end of a base word. **Ed** is a suffix.

dan **ger** — **G** may say /j/ before **e**.

2   3
dr**ead** ful — When full is a suffix, it loses an **l**.

m**o**st — Underline /ō/. **O** may say /ō/ when followed by two consonants. [Note: This is a spelling rule, so we do not write a number above the vowel. See "Analyzing the Spelling Words" in the the instructions for Part 2.]

an **y** **thing** — This is a compound word. Underline **y**. Vowel **y** says /ē/ at the end of a multi-syllable word.

p**urr**   pa**th**

af **ter** n**oo**n   pump

p**ow** **er**   cl**ear**

dip p<u>er</u>   The base word is one syllable and ends in one vowel followed by one consonant, so we double the final consonant before adding a vowel suffix.

<u>th</u> <u>i</u>rst y   Underline **y**. Vowel **y** says /ē/ at the end of a multi-syllable word.

r<u>e</u> mem b<u>er</u>   Underline /ē/; **e** says /ē/ at the end of a syllable. [Note: This word has a lazy vowel. See "Sounding Out and Lazy Vowels" in the instructions for Part 2.]

sp<u>ar</u> kling   When adding a vowel suffix, we drop the final silent **e** from the base word if it is no longer needed.

d<u>i</u> <u>a</u> monds^2 Underline /ī/; **i** says /ī/ at the end of a syllable. Underline /ā/; **a** says /ā/ at the end of a syllable.

^{3}

stre<u>tch</u> <u>ed</u>   Phonogram **tch** is used only after a single vowel which does not say its name.

m<u>i</u>nd   Underline /ī/. **I** may say /ī/ when followed by two consonants.

f<u>ier</u><u>ce</u>$_{=3}$ **C** says /s/ because of the silent **e**; underline the **c**, and double underline the silent **e**.

ex press   We often double /s/ after a single vowel at the end of a base word.

qu <u>ee</u>r   can not   d<u>ee</u>ds

$^{2\ \ 2}$ ^{2} ^{2}
p<u>oured</u>   hap pen<u>ed</u>   an o<u>th</u> er

prin cess   *C* says /s/ before *e*. We often double /s/ after a single vowel at the end of a base word.

dance₌₃   *C* says /s/ because of the silent *e*; underline the *c*, and double underline the silent *e*.

skies   Vowel *y* changes to *i* before adding any ending unless the ending begins with *i*.

min ute₌₅   Double underline the silent *e*.

course₌₅   Double underline the silent *e*.

gate keep er   This is a compound word. *A* says /ā/ because of the silent *e*; underline the silent *e* twice, and draw a bridge between the silent *e* and the *a*.

save   *A* says /ā/ because of the silent *e*; underline the silent *e* twice, and draw a bridge between the silent *e* and the *a*. English words do not end in *v*; underline the *v*.

share   *A* says /ā/ because of the silent *e*; underline the silent *e* twice, and draw a bridge between the silent *e* and the *a*.

ze ro   Underline /ē/; *e* says /ē/ at the end of a syllable. Underline /ō/; *o* says /ō/ at the end of a syllable.

bloomed   yes ter day

pound   sear ch ing

news   help ers

naug<u>h</u> t<u>y</u> Underline **y**. Vowel **y** says /ē/ at the end of a multi-syllable word.

<u>o</u> h<u>o</u> Underline /ō/; **o** says /ō/ at the end of a syllable.

qui<u>ck</u> ness Phonogram **ck** is used only after a single vowel which says its first sound.

g<u>a</u>²<u>th</u> <u>er</u>² ed

moss We often double /s/ after a single vowel at the end of a base word.

fen<u>c</u><u>e</u>₌₃ **C** says /s/ because of the silent **e**; underline the **c**, and double underline the silent **e**.

st<u>oo</u>²d

to w<u>ar</u>³d

str<u>ea</u>m

n<u>ei</u>² <u>th</u> <u>er</u>²

streng <u>th</u>

f<u>ar</u> <u>th</u>² er

mad

gr<u>oa</u>n

led

use
(2)

U says /ū/ because of the silent *e*; underline the silent *e* twice, and draw a bridge between the silent *e* and the *u*.

but ter cup

This is a compound word.

ar rant

Definition: utter or complete. [Note: Not the phonogram *ar*, /ǎ-r/.]

snuff<u>ed</u>
(3)

We often double /f/ after a single vowel at the end of a base word. Phonogram *ed* is a suffix.

h<u>o</u>ld

Underline /ō/. *O* may say /ō/ when followed by two consonants.

br<u>ea</u>k fast
(3)

This is a compound word. The word literally means to break one's fast after waking.

bat tle
(=4)

Every syllable must have a written vowel; double underline the silent *e*.

e<u>dge</u>

Phonogram *dge* is used only after a single vowel which says its first sound.

le<u>dge</u>

Phonogram *dge* is used only after a single vowel which says its first sound.

h<u>ee</u>ls
(2)

fun ni[3] est   Vowel *y* changes to *i* before adding any ending unless the ending begins with *i*.

tapp<u>ed</u>[3]   The base word is one syllable and ends in one vowel followed by one consonant, so we double the final consonant before adding a vowel suffix.

left

prop <u>er</u>

<u>which</u>

pi<u>e</u> <u>ce</u>₌₃ **C** says /s/ because of the silent **e**; underline the **c**, and double underline the silent **e**. Memory tip: a piece of PIE. If desired, use a colored pencil to underline PIE.

²
<u>wh</u> <u>ee</u>l b<u>ar</u> r<u>ow</u> This is a compound word.

²
kill<u>ed</u> We often double /l/ after a single vowel at the end of a base word. Phonogram **ed** is a suffix.

⁴   ²
tr<u>ou</u> bl<u>es</u>₌₄ Every syllable must have a written vowel; double underline the silent **e**.

c<u>ar</u> r<u>y</u> <u>ing</u> Underline **y**. Vowel **y** says /ē/ at the end of a multi-syllable base word. **Ing** is a suffix.

² ²
<u>th</u>ōs<u>e</u> **O** says /ō/ because of the silent **e**; underline the silent **e** twice, and draw a bridge between the silent **e** and the **o**.

cl<u>i</u> māt<u>e</u> Underline /ī/; **i** says /ī/ at the end of a syllable. **A** says /ā/ because of the silent **e**; underline the silent **e** twice, and draw a bridge between the silent **e** and the **a**.

²
<u>sh</u> <u>oul</u> d<u>er</u>   fed

²
d<u>ough</u>   mut ton

ov en   dr<u>aw</u>

ram   dr<u>ew</u>

ch arm ing ly   Underline **y**. Vowel **y** says /ē/ at the end of a multi-syllable word.

ter ri bly   Underline **y**. Vowel **y** says /ē/ at the end of a multi-syllable word.

a like   Underline /ā/; **a** says /ā/ at the end of a syllable. **I** says /ī/ because of the silent **e**; underline the silent **e** twice, and draw a bridge between the silent **e** and the **i**.

a gainst   Underline /ā/; **a** says /ā/ at the end of a syllable.

struck   Phonogram **ck** is used only after a single vowel which says its first sound.

lo cal   Underline /ō/; **o** says /ō/ at the end of a syllable.

³false₅   Double underline the silent **e**.

²ch eese₅   Double underline the silent **e**.

trod den   The base word is one syllable and ends in one vowel followed by one consonant, so we double the final consonant before adding a vowel suffix.

hea th

²curled

su<u>i</u>ts

g<u>lor</u> y

Underline **y**. Vowel **y** says /ē/ at the end of a multi-syllable word. [Note: This is an abnormal syllabification to avoid breaking apart an obvious phonogram.]

²
lin <u>ing</u>

When adding a vowel suffix, we drop the final silent **e** from the base word if it is no longer needed.

^{2 2}
l<u>ined</u>

When adding a vowel suffix, we drop the final silent **e** from the base word if it is no longer needed. In this case, we drop the **e** and add **ed**.

In the two last words, we added vowel suffixes to the base word "line." In both cases, the rule is that we drop the final silent **e** from the base word before adding the vowel suffix. We say this even when the base word already ends with **e** because this keeps the rule simple. There are a number of vowel suffixes which begin with **e**, such as **ed**, **en**, **er**, and **es**, and our basic rule works for these even though it means we're dropping an **e** and adding another one. This way, we don't have to have one rule for suffixes that begin with **e** and another rule for suffixes that begin with other vowels. One rule works for all of the vowel suffixes.

grass hop per — This is a compound word. We often double /s/ after a single vowel at the end of a base word. The base word "hop" is one syllable and ends in one vowel followed by one consonant, so we double the final consonant before adding a vowel suffix.

same — *A* says /ā/ because of the silent *e*; underline the silent *e* twice, and draw a bridge between the silent *e* and the *a*.

stiff — We often double /f/ after a single vowel at the end of a base word.

kind ness — Underline /ī/. *I* may say /ī/ when followed by two consonants.

feed

our selves — Double underline the silent *e*. To make the word "self" plural, use *v* instead of *f* and add *es*.

huff — We often double /f/ after a single vowel at the end of a base word.

gab bling — When adding a vowel suffix, we drop the final silent *e* from the base word if it is no longer needed; silent *e* provided the written vowel for the syllable.

c<u>oa</u>l

fa<u>sh</u>⁴ ion   Think to spell /făsh-yŏn/.

h<u>ow</u> ev <u>er</u>

<u>work</u> <u>er</u>

h<u>ar</u>m

m<u>ea</u>l

r<u>oa</u>st <u>ed</u>   Phonogram **ed** forms a new syllable when the base word ends in **d** or **t**.

frog

an i mal
（3 above i）

h<u>er</u> self

strang<u>e</u>
(bridge over a...e)

A says /ā/ because of the silent **e**; underline the silent **e** twice, and draw a bridge between the silent **e** and the **a**. **G** says /j/ because of the silent **e**; underline the **g**.

s<u>ou</u>p
(3 above)

w<u>ealth</u> <u>y</u>
(2 above)

Underline **y**. Vowel **y** says /ē/ at the end of a multi-syllable word.

snug

<u>wr</u>ong

t<u>ow</u> <u>er</u>

r<u>ope</u>
(bridge over o...e)

O says /ō/ because of the silent **e**; underline the silent **e** twice, and draw a bridge between the silent **e** and the **o**.

ring

ran<u>g</u>

flat

<u>sh</u>ot

gas

pole   **O** says /ō/ because of the silent **e**; underline the silent **e** twice, and draw a bridge between the silent **e** and the **o**.

car ried   Vowel **y** changes to **i** before adding any ending unless the ending begins with **i**.
Alternatively: **I** says /ē/; mark it with a 4.
Underline phonogram **ed**; mark it with a 2.

un tie   **I** says /ī/ because of the silent **e**; underline the silent **e** twice, and draw a bridge between the silent **e** and the **i**. **Un** is a prefix.

drive   **I** says /ī/ because of the silent **e**; underline the silent **e** twice, and draw a bridge between the silent **e** and the **i**. English words do not end in v; underline the v.

no bod y   This is a compound word. Underline /ō/; **o** says /ō/ at the end of a syllable. Underline **y**. Vowel **y** says /ē/ at the end of a multi-syllable word.

word

war

wher ev er   This is a compound word.

un less   We often double /s/ after a single vowel at the end of a base word.

bad

st<u>a</u> bl<u>e</u>=4	Underline /ā/; *a* says /ā/ at the end of a syllable. Every syllable must have a written vowel; double underline the silent *e*.
b<u>a</u> con 3 salt	Underline /ā/; *a* says /ā/ at the end of a syllable.
ston<u>e</u>	*O* says /ō/ because of the silent *e*; underline the silent *e* twice, and draw a bridge between the silent *e* and the *o*.
self i<u>sh</u>	

$\overset{2}{\text{man}}$ g<u>er</u>   G may say /j/ before **e**.

<u>ough</u>t

star <u>ve</u>$_{\underset{=}{2}}$ English words do not end in **v**; underline the **v**, and double underline the silent **e**.

st<u>ar</u>v <u>ing</u>   When adding a vowel suffix, we drop the final silent **e** from the base word if it is no longer needed; silent **e** kept the word from ending in **v**.

lif<u><u>e</u></u>   **I** says /ī/ because of the silent **e**; underline the silent **e** twice, and draw a bridge between the silent **e** and the **i**.

els<u>e</u>$_{=5}$ Double underline the silent **e**.

b<u>e</u> l<u>ongs</u>   Underline /ē/; **e** says /ē/ at the end of a syllable.

cas tl<u>e</u>$_{==4}$ Double underline the silent **t**. Every syllable must have a written vowel; double underline the silent **e**.

$\overset{2}{\text{mak}}$ <u>er</u>   When adding a vowel suffix, we drop the final silent **e** from the base word if it is no longer needed. In this case, we drop the **e** and add **er**.

$\overset{2}{\text{se}}$<u>a</u> son

ĭc͜e̲

I says /ī/ because of the silent *e*; underline the silent *e* twice, and draw a bridge between the silent *e* and the *i*. *C* says /s/ because of the silent *e*; underline the *c*.

lăc͜e̲

A says /ā/ because of the silent *e*; underline the silent *e* twice, and draw a bridge between the silent *e* and the *a*. *C* says /s/ because of the silent *e*; underline the *c*.

băr͜e̲

A says /ā/ because of the silent *e*; underline the silent *e* twice, and draw a bridge between the silent *e* and the *a*.

zip

dad dy̲

The base word is one syllable and ends in one vowel followed by one consonant, so we double the final consonant before adding a vowel suffix. Underline *y*. Vowel *y* says /ē/ at the end of a multi-syllable word.

strắng e͟r͟s   G may say /j/ before *e*.

mine͟   *I* says /ī/ because of the silent *e*; underline the silent *e* twice, and draw a bridge between the silent *e* and the *i*.

qui͟c͟k   Phonogram ***ck*** is used only after a single vowel which says its first sound.

gen tle͟   G may say /j/ before *e*. Every syllable must have a written vowel; double underline the silent *e*.

lis te͟n   Double underline the silent *t*.

mo͟ve͟   English words do not end in *v*; underline the *v*, and double underline the silent *e*.

wi͟ld   Underline /ī/. *I* may say /ī/ when followed by two consonants.

f͟u͟r   lo͟r͟d

spe͟a͟k   o͟i͟l

so͟u͟nd   pe͟r͟ c͟h͟

fe͟a͟st   c͟h͟in

pass

We often double /s/ after a single vowel at the end of a base word.

ro<u>ck</u>

Phonogram **ck** is used only after a single vowel which says its first sound.

fu<u>dge</u>

Phonogram **dge** is used only after a single vowel which says its first sound.

fun n<u>y</u>

The base word is one syllable and ends in one vowel followed by one consonant, so we double the final consonant before adding a vowel suffix. Underline **y**. Vowel **y** says /ē/ at the end of a multi-syllable word.

cr<u>ea</u>m

t<u>ar</u>t

³ ²
wan d<u>er</u>s

²
l<u>ow</u> ing

str<u>ay</u>

²
bl<u>ow</u>n

fists

²
sh <u>ow</u> <u>er</u>s

jump <u>er</u>

br<u>ea</u> <u>th</u>

³
gr<u>ou</u>p

161

tur tle$_{=4}$ Every syllable must have a written vowel; double underline the silent **e**.

fish er man   This is a compound word.

te$\overset{2}{as}$ ing   When adding a vowel suffix, we drop the final silent **e** from the base word if it is no longer needed.

te$\overset{2}{as}$e$\overset{2}{d}$ When adding a vowel suffix, we drop the final silent **e** from the base word if it is no longer needed. In this case, we drop the **e** and add **ed**.

stroke   **O** says /ō/ because of the silent **e**; underline the silent **e** twice, and draw a bridge between the silent **e** and the **o**.

th $\overset{2}{ou}$ sand

s$\overset{2}{av}$ ing   When adding a vowel suffix, we drop the final silent **e** from the base word if it is no longer needed; silent **e** kept the word from ending in **v**.

king

pal ace$_{=3}$ **C** says /s/ because of the silent **e**; underline the **c**, and double underline the silent **e**.

bot tom

spar kle₌₄   Every syllable must have a written vowel; double underline the silent **e**.

since₌₃   **C** says /s/ because of the silent **e**; underline the **c**, and double underline the silent **e**.

e lev en   Underline /ē/; **e** says /ē/ at the end of a syllable.

doc tor

inch

cli̲mb

Underline /ī/. *I* may say /ī/ when followed by two consonants.

a̲ gre̲e̲

Underline /ā/; *a* says /ā/ at the end of a syllable.

jou̲r ney²

Our is an advanced phonogram which says /er/.

me̲a̲² su̲re̲₌₅²

Underline the silent *e* twice.
Alternatively: *U* says /ū/ because of the silent *e*; underline the silent *e* twice, and draw a bridge between the silent *e* and the *u*.

bree̲ze̲₌₅

Double underline the silent *e*.

role̲₌

O says /ō/ because of the silent *e*; underline the silent *e* twice, and draw a bridge between the silent *e* and the *o*.

strīke̲₌

I says /ī/ because of the silent *e*; underline the silent *e* twice, and draw a bridge between the silent *e* and the *i*.

pi̲c̲k̲

Phonogram *ck* is used only after a single vowel which says its first sound.

el e pha̲nt

spu̲r

trunk

tou̲ ch̲⁴ ed̲³

mon key̲²

ru̲sh̲ ed̲³

qu ar̲ rel

up st<u>ai</u>rs   This is a compound word.

s<u>o</u>l di<u>er</u>   Pronounced /sōl-jer/. Think to spell /sōld-yer/.
^{4 above o}   Underline /ō/. **O** may say /ō/ when followed by
        two consonants.

tame   **A** says /ā/ because of the silent **e**; underline the
        silent **e** twice, and draw a bridge between the
        silent **e** and the **a**.

mar ch

blo<u>ck</u>   Phonogram **ck** is used only after a single vowel
        which says its first sound.

inn   We sometimes double a consonant after a single
        vowel at the end of a base word.

smile   **I** says /ī/ because of the silent **e**; underline the
        silent **e** twice, and draw a bridge between the
        silent **e** and the **i**.

f<u>or</u> give=2   This is a compound word. English words do not
        end in **v**; underline the **v**, and double underline
        the silent **e**.

gun   fond

tramp   rap

b<u>ear</u>   won
²

t<u>ea</u>rs

f<u>o</u>ld — Underline /ō/. **O** may say /ō/ when followed by two consonants.

lat<u>e</u> — **A** says /ā/ because of the silent **e**; underline the silent **e** twice, and draw a bridge between the silent **e** and the **a**.

twin

twi<u>ce</u> — **I** says /ī/ because of the silent **e**; underline the silent **e** twice, and draw a bridge between the silent **e** and the **i**. **C** says /s/ because of the silent **e**; underline the **c**.

twen t<u>y</u> — Underline **y**. Vowel **y** says /ē/ at the end of a multi-syllable word.

twel<u>ve</u>₌₂ — English words do not end in **v**; underline the **v**, and double underline the silent **e**.

twelf<u>th</u>

liv <u>ing</u> — When adding a vowel suffix, we drop the final silent **e** from the base word if it is no longer needed; silent **e** kept the word from ending in **v**.

bl<u>ea</u>t   <u>ea</u>rn

spar r<u>ow</u>²   str<u>aw</u>

t<u>ea</u> <u>ch</u>   af t<u>er</u> w<u>ar</u>ds²

tau<u>gh</u>t

hur ry ing — Underline *y*. Vowel *y* says /ē/ at the end of a multi-syllable base word. ***Ing*** is a suffix.

cer tain — C says /s/ before *e*.

ex cept — C says /s/ before *e*.

cloud y — Underline *y*. Vowel *y* says /ē/ at the end of a multi-syllable word.

male — ***A*** says /ā/ because of the silent *e*; underline the silent *e* twice, and draw a bridge between the silent *e* and the *a*.

fe male — Underline /ē/; *e* says /ē/ at the end of a syllable. ***A*** says /ā/ because of the silent *e*; underline the silent *e* twice, and draw a bridge between the silent *e* and the *a*.

sum ma ry — Underline *y*. Vowel *y* says /ē/ at the end of a multi-syllable word.

lov ing — When adding a vowel suffix, we drop the final silent *e* from the base word if it is no longer needed; silent *e* kept the word from ending in *v*.

swal low

fol low

ch urn

bought

heat

lid

vis it

cap

cape *A* says /ā/ because of the silent *e*; underline the silent *e* twice, and draw a bridge between the silent *e* and the *a*.

cit y C says /s/ before *i*. Underline *y*. Vowel *y* says /ē/ at the end of a multi-syllable word.

cit ies C says /s/ before *i*. Vowel *y* changes to *i* before adding any ending unless the ending begins with *i*.

bak ing When adding a vowel suffix, we drop the final silent *e* from the base word if it is no longer needed.

wore Double underline the silent *e*.
Alternatively: *O* says /ō/ because of the silent *e*; underline the silent *e* twice, and draw a bridge between the silent *e* and the *o*.

wood peck er Phonogram *ck* is used only after a single vowel which says its first sound.

ch airs

pinch ed

cen ter C says /s/ before *e*.

ta ble
   =4

Underline /ā/; a says /ā/ at the end of a syllable. Every syllable must have a written vowel; double underline the silent *e*.

sur prise

I says /ī/ because of the silent *e*; underline the silent *e* twice, and draw a bridge between the silent *e* and the *i*.

cleanse
      =5

Double underline the silent *e*.

some one
   =5

This is a compound word. Some: Double underline the silent *e*. One: This is an exception. Think to spell /ōn/, say /won/.

ser vants

95

se cret   Underline /ē/; **e** says /ē/ at the end of a syllable.

cher ry   Underline **y**. Vowel **y** says /ē/ at the end of a multi-syllable word.

shan't   Contraction for "shall not."

chil ly   Underline **y**. Vowel **y** says /ē/ at the end of a multi-syllable word.

whole   **Wh** says /h/. Put a small X to show that it's an eXception. **O** says /ō/ because of the silent **e**; underline the silent **e** twice, and draw a bridge between the silent **e** and the **o**.

tone   **O** says /ō/ because of the silent **e**; underline the silent **e** twice, and draw a bridge between the silent **e** and the **o**.

trem bling   When adding a vowel suffix, we drop the final silent **e** from the base word if it is no longer needed; silent **e** provided the written vowel for the syllable.

po sies   Underline /ō/; **o** says /ō/ at the end of a syllable.

rod   wh irl ing

pod   test

ends   frost

nor

skat͡e̲s · *A* says /ā/ because of the silent *e*; underline the silent *e* twice, and draw a bridge between the silent *e* and the *a*.

i̲ vo̲ ry̲ · Underline /ī/; *i* says /ī/ at the end of a syllable. Underline /ō/; *o* says /ō/ at the end of a syllable. Underline *y*. Vowel *y* says /ē/ at the end of a multi-syllable word.

bas͡e̲ · *A* says /ā/ because of the silent *e*; underline the silent *e* twice, and draw a bridge between the silent *e* and the *a*.

we̲ak

grav͡e̲ · *A* says /ā/ because of the silent *e*; underline the silent *e* twice, and draw a bridge between the silent *e* and the *a*. English words do not end in *v*; underline the *v*.

a̲rm ful³ · When full is a suffix, it loses an *l*.

kit tie̲s² · Vowel *y* changes to *i* before adding any ending unless the ending begins with *i*.

we̲a th̲ er² ²	wil lo̲w²
hon ey̲²	cle̲an
hum	sh̲eets
mon th̲s	sleds²

mag pie⌒ *I* says /ī/ because of the silent *e*; underline the silent *e* twice, and draw a bridge between the silent *e* and the *i*.

shape⌒ *A* says /ā/ because of the silent *e*; underline the silent *e* twice, and draw a bridge between the silent *e* and the *a*.

spoke⌒ *O* says /ō/ because of the silent *e*; underline the silent *e* twice, and draw a bridge between the silent *e* and the *o*.

²ease₌₅ Double underline the silent *e*.

wind Homograph: wīnd.

sticks Phonogram *ck* is used only after a single vowel which says its first sound.

sit ting The base word is one syllable and ends in one vowel followed by one consonant, so we double the final consonant before adding a vowel suffix.

les son   hoot

mud   cot ton

thrush   ³to mor ²row

²twigs   ²peas

172

p<u>or</u> c<u>u</u> pīn<u>e</u>	Underline /ū/; **u** says /ū/ at the end of a syllable. I says /ī/ because of the silent **e**; underline the silent **e** twice, and draw a bridge between the silent **e** and the i.
l<u>arge</u>₃	**G** says /j/ because of the silent **e**; underline the **g**, and double underline the silent **e**.
cel l<u>ar</u>	C says /s/ before **e**.
crīm<u>e</u>	**I** says /ī/ because of the silent **e**; underline the silent **e** twice, and draw a bridge between the silent **e** and the **i**.
ki<u>tch</u> en	Phonogram **tch** is used only after a single vowel which does not say its name.
³kno<u>ck</u> ed	Phonogram **ck** is used only after a single vowel which says its first sound.

hog	fr<u>ee</u> dom
t<u>igh</u>t	gift
di<u>sh</u>	t<u>oo</u> <u>th</u>
st<u>ew</u>	t<u>ee</u> <u>th</u>
sent	
bump	

X 2
wolv<u>e</u><u>s</u>   **O** says /ü/. Put a small X to show that it's an eXception. Double underline the silent **e**. To make the word wolf plural, change the **f** to **v** and add **es**.

h<u>e</u> r<u>o</u>   Underline /ē/; **e** says /ē/ at the end of a syllable. Underline /ō/; **o** says /ō/ at the end of a syllable.

t<u>i</u> tl<u>e</u>   Underline /ī/; **i** says /ī/ at the end of a syllable.
=4   Every syllable must have a written vowel; double underline the silent **e**.

g<u>i</u> ant   **G** may say /j/ before **i**. Underline /ī/; **i** says /ī/ at the end of a syllable.

l<u>i</u> on   Underline /ī/; **i** says /ī/ at the end of a syllable.

wi<u>tch</u>   Phonogram **tch** is used only after a single vowel which does not say its name.

3
pe<u>ck</u> <u>ed</u>   Phonogram **ck** is used only after a single vowel which says its first sound.

ben<u>ch</u>   ex pect i<u>ng</u>

3
nipp<u>ed</u>   p<u>er</u> haps

3
snipp<u>ed</u>   pa<u>i</u>d

3
snapp<u>ed</u>   2
                             neigh b<u>or</u>s

100

judge — Phonogram **dge** is used only after a single vowel which says its first sound.

robes [2] — **O** says /ō/ because of the silent **e**; underline the silent **e** twice, and draw a bridge between the silent **e** and the **o**.

lame — **A** says /ā/ because of the silent **e**; underline the silent **e** twice, and draw a bridge between the silent **e** and the **a**.

[3] al most — When all is a prefix, it loses an **l**. Underline /ō/. **O** may say /ō/ when followed by two consonants.

blind — Underline /ī/. **I** may say /ī/ when followed by two consonants.

mo ment — Underline /ō/; **o** says /ō/ at the end of a syllable.

a mount — Underline /ā/; **a** says /ā/ at the end of a syllable.

rung — front

thin — steps

nap — join

pun ish — al low

d<u>ee</u>r

b<u>o</u>²<u>w</u>   Homograph: b<u>o</u><u>w.</u>

ar r<u>o</u>²<u>w</u>

fing <u>er</u>²s   [Note: This is an abnormal syllabification to
                     avoid breaking apart an obvious phonogram.]
nu<u>mb</u>

<u>ch</u> <u>ar</u> g<u>e</u>=3   **G** says /j/ because of the silent **e**; underline the
                     g, and double underline the silent **e**.

wig w3ăm

mag ic   G may say /j/ before **i**.

m<u>ee</u>t   Definition: to get together or be introduced
                     to someone.

ot t<u>er</u>

b<u>ea</u> v<u>er</u>

ba<u>dg</u> <u>er</u>   Phonograms **dge** and **er** share the **e** in this
                     word, so it can be underlined with two different
                     phonograms. Alternatively, G may say /j/ before **e**.

ex pens<u>e</u>=5   Double underline the silent **e**.

fif<u>th</u>

in f<u>or</u> m<u>a</u> <u>ti</u>on   Underline /ā/; **a** says /ā/ at the end of
                     a syllable.

bri<u>ck</u>s Phonogram **ck** is used only after a single vowel which says its first sound.

ju<u>ic</u> <u>y</u> C says /s/ before **y**. When adding a vowel suffix, we drop the final silent **e** from the base word if it is no longer needed.

<u>o</u>'clo<u>ck</u> Contraction for "of the clock." Underline /ō/; **o** says /ō/ at the end of a syllable. Phonogram **ck** is used only after a single vowel which says its first sound.

the<u>se</u> **E** says /ē/ because of the silent **e**; underline the silent **e** twice, and draw a bridge between the silent **e** and the **e**.

pi<u>e</u> **I** says /ī/ because of the silent **e**; underline the silent **e** twice, and draw a bridge between the silent **e** and the **i**.

des s<u>er</u>t Definition: sweet treat at the end of the meal.

<u>u</u> s<u>u</u> al Underline /ū/; **u** says /ū/ at the end of a syllable.

d<u>e</u> st<u>ro</u>y Underline /ē/; **e** says /ē/ at the end of a syllable.

d<u>i</u> rec <u>tion</u> Underline /ī/; **i** says /ī/ at the end of a syllable.

r<u>ai</u> sins   r<u>ows</u>

vis i t<u>or</u>s   f<u>air</u>

scat t<u>er</u> <u>ed</u>   <u>th</u> <u>ir</u>d

wife

I says /ī/ because of the silent *e*; underline the silent *e* twice, and draw a bridge between the silent *e* and the *i*.

lose

Double underline the silent *e*.

hear th

Double underline the silent *e*.

plate

A says /ā/ because of the silent *e*; underline the silent *e* twice, and draw a bridge between the silent *e* and the *a*.

care ful

A says /ā/ because of the silent *e*; underline the silent *e* twice, and draw a bridge between the silent *e* and the *a*. When full is a suffix, it loses an *l*.

latch

Phonogram *tch* is used only after a single vowel which does not say its name.

speck led

Phonogram *ck* is used only after a single vowel which says its first sound. When adding a vowel suffix, we drop the final silent *e* from the base word if it is no longer needed; silent *e* provided the written vowel for the syllable.

cut ter

The base word is one syllable and ends in one vowel followed by one consonant, so we double the final consonant before adding a vowel suffix.

noon

pink

lift <u>ed</u>   Phonogram **ed** forms a new syllable when the
                        base word ends in **d** or **t**.

in f<u>or</u>m

f<u>our</u>th²

m<u>ea</u>nt²

leng<u>th</u>

pan try	Underline **y**. Vowel **y** says /ē/ at the end of a multi-syllable word.
true₌₂	Underline /ū/; **u** says /ū/ at the end of a syllable. English words do not end in **u**; underline the **u**, and double underline the silent **e**.
be lie ve₌₂	Underline /ē/; **e** says /ē/ at the end of a syllable. English words do not end in **v**; underline the **v**, and double underline the silent **e**.
prob a bly	Underline **y**. Vowel **y** says /ē/ at the end of a multi-syllable word.
re quest	Underline /ē/; **e** says /ē/ at the end of a syllable.
them² selves²	Double underline the silent **e**. To make the word "self" plural, use **v** instead of **f** and add **es**.
ser ve₌₂	English words do not end in **v**; underline the **v**, and double underline the silent **e**.
clothes²	**O** says /ō/ because of the silent **e**; underline the silent **e** twice, and draw a bridge between the silent **e** and the **o**.
lad	
spread²	
in stead²	

180

<u>wor</u> <u>th</u>

crust

maȱk² <u>ing</u>   When adding a vowel suffix, we drop the final silent *e* from the base word if it is no longer needed.

fel lo̤w²

The next twelve words are the months of the year. They are in order, so you'll be able to memorize them while you practice reading them. The names of the months are proper names, so each name begins with a capital letter.

Jan u ar y   [Note: Not the **ar** phonogram. Think to spell with the first sound, /ă-r/.]
Underline /ū/; **u** says /ū/ at the end of a syllable. Underline **y**. Vowel **y** says /ē/ at the end of a multi-syllable word.

Feb ru ar y   [Note: Not the **ar** phonogram. Think to spell with the first sound, /ă-r/.]
Underline /ū/; **u** says /ū/ at the end of a syllable. Underline **y**. Vowel **y** says /ē/ at the end of a multi-syllable word.

Mar ch

A pril   Underline /ā/; a says /ā/ at the end of a syllable.

May

June   **U** says /ū/ because of the silent **e**; underline the silent **e** twice, and draw a bridge between the silent **e** and the **u**.

Ju ly³   Underline /ū/; **u** says /ū/ at the end of a syllable.

Au gust

Sep tem ber

Oc to ber

Underline /ō/; **o** says /ō/ at the end of a syllable.

No vem ber

Underline /ō/; **o** says /ō/ at the end of a syllable.

De cem ber

Underline /ē/; **e** says /ē/ at the end of a syllable. C says /s/ before **e**.

cal en dar

month

dec ade

A says /ā/ because of the silent **e**; underline the silent **e** twice, and draw a bridge between the silent **e** and the **a**.

<u>ear</u> <u>th</u> <u>y</u>   Underline *y*. Vowel *y* says /ē/ at the end of a multi-syllable word.

³ ²
halls   We often double /l/ after a single vowel at the end of a base word. *S* is an ending that makes hall plural.

t<u>ee</u> n<u>y</u>   Underline *y*. Vowel *y* says /ē/ at the end of a multi-syllable word.

cr<u>aw</u>l <u>y</u>   Underline *y*. Vowel *y* says /ē/ at the end of a multi-syllable word.

<u>ar</u> rán<u>ge</u>   *A* says /ā/ because of the silent *e*; underline the silent *e* twice, and draw a bridge between the silent *e* and the *a*. *G* says /j/ because of the silent *e*; underline the *g*.

sim pl<u>y</u>   Underline *y*. Vowel *y* says /ē/ at the end of a multi-syllable word.

³
<u>aw</u> ful   When full is a suffix, it loses an *l*.

en tir<u>e</u>   *I* says /ī/ because of the silent *e*; underline the silent *e* twice, and draw a bridge between the silent *e* and the *i*.

flut <u>ter</u> <u>ing</u>   trum pet

con tent   ³
        wand

blan ket   si<u>gh</u>

²
col <u>ors</u>

face — **A** says /ā/ because of the silent **e**; underline the silent **e** twice, and draw a bridge between the silent **e** and the **a**. **C** says /s/ because of the silent **e**; underline the **c**.

fac ed — C says /s/ before **e**. When adding a vowel suffix, we drop the final silent **e** from the base word if it is no longer needed.

pale — **A** says /ā/ because of the silent **e**; underline the silent **e** twice, and draw a bridge between the silent **e** and the **a**.

froz en — When adding a vowel suffix, we drop the final silent **e** from the base word if it is no longer needed. In this case, we drop the **e** and add **en**.

few

com plete — **E** says /ē/ because of the silent **e**; underline the silent **e** twice, and draw a bridge between the silent **e** and the **e**.

com plete ly — **E** says /ē/ because of the silent **e**; underline the silent **e** twice, and draw a bridge between the silent **e** and the **e**. Underline **y**. Vowel **y** says /ē/ at the end of a multi-syllable word.

fai th ful — When full is a suffix, it loses an **l**.

<u>a</u> p<u>ar</u>t   Underline /ā/; *a* says /ā/ at the end of a syllable.

wh<u>ine͡s</u>²

²
wad <u>ed</u>   When adding a vowel suffix, we drop the final silent *e* from the base word if it is no longer needed. Phonogram *ed* forms a new syllable when the base word ends in *d* or *t*.

sank

mer͡<u>e</u>   *E* says /ē/ because of the silent *e*; underline the silent *e* twice, and draw a bridge between the silent *e* and the *e*.

pri͡c<u>e</u>   *I* says /ī/ because of the silent *e*; underline the silent *e* twice, and draw a bridge between the silent *e* and the *i*. *C* says /s/ because of the silent *e*; underline the *c*.

f<u>or</u> t<u>y</u>   Underline *y*. Vowel *y* says /ē/ at the end of a multi-syllable word.

108

broom

vase

A says /ā/ because of the silent e; underline the silent e twice, and draw a bridge between the silent e and the a.

nap kins

knife

I says /ī/ because of the silent e; underline the silent e twice, and draw a bridge between the silent e and the i.

tea spoon

carved

When adding a vowel suffix, we drop the final silent e from the base word if it is no longer needed; silent e kept the word from ending in v.

meat

po ta to

Underline /ō/; o says /ō/ at the end of a syllable.
Underline /ā/; a says /ā/ at the end of a syllable.

po ta toes

Underline /ō/; o says /ō/ at the end of a syllable.
Underline /ā/; a says /ā/ at the end of a syllable.
Words that end in o often form the plural by adding es.

cran ber ry

Underline y. Vowel y says /ē/ at the end of a multi-syllable word.

sau <u>ce</u>=3   **C** says /s/ because of the silent **e**; underline the **c**, and double underline the silent **e**.

3
squa<u>sh</u>

X2
bus <u>y</u>   **U** says /ĭ/. Put a small X to show that it's an eXception.

X2
bus i ness   Abnormal syllabication. Say /biz-ness/, but think to spell /bĭz-ĭ-ness/. **U** says /ĭ/. Put a small X to show that it's an eXception.

pr<u>e</u> f<u>er</u>   **E** says /ē/ because of the silent **e**; underline the silent **e** twice, and draw a bridge between the silent **e** and the **e**.

cob webs

trimm²ed   The base word is one syllable and ends in one vowel followed by one consonant, so we double the final consonant before adding a vowel suffix.

pop corn   This is a compound word.

can d²ies   Vowel *y* changes to *i* before adding any ending unless the ending begins with *i*.

toys

lock³ ed   Phonogram *ck* is used only after a single vowel which says its first sound.

al read y   Underline *y*. Vowel *y* says /ē/ at the end of a multi-syllable word. When all is a prefix, it loses an *l*.

ca nar y   Underline *y*. Vowel *y* says /ē/ at the end of a multi-syllable word.

spi der   Underline /ī/; *i* says /ī/ at the end of a syllable.

at tic

poke   *O* says /ō/ because of the silent *e*; underline the silent *e* twice, and draw a bridge between the silent *e* and the *o*.

sing l<u>e</u>₄ Every syllable must have a written vowel; double underline the silent *e*.

f<u>i</u> nal l<u>y</u> Underline /ī/; *i* says /ī/ at the end of a syllable.

m<u>o</u> t<u>i</u>on Underline /ō/; *o* says /ō/ at the end of a syllable.

ro<u>y</u> al

The next nine words are the names of the planets in our solar system, including the dwarf planet Pluto. They are in order, so you'll be able to memorize them while you practice reading them. The names of the planets are proper names, so each name begins with a capital letter.

Mer cu ry   Underline /ū/; *u* says /ū/ at the end of a syllable. Underline *y*. Vowel *y* says /ē/ at the end of a multi-syllable word.

Ve nus   Underline /ē/; *e* says /ē/ at the end of a syllable.

Ear th

2
Mars

Ju pi ter   Underline /ū/; *u* says /ū/ at the end of a syllable.

Sat urn

2
Ur a nus

Nep tune   *U* says /ū/ because of the silent *e*; underline the silent *e* twice, and draw a bridge between the silent *e* and the *u*.

Plu to   Underline /ū/; *u* says /ū/ at the end of a syllable. Underline /ō/; *o* says /ō/ at the end of a syllable.

plan ets

2   2
h<u>ea</u> vens

dis tan<u>c</u><u>e</u>₃	*C* says /s/ because of the silent *e*; underline the *c*, and double underline the silent *e*.
s<u>e</u> lect	Underline /ē/; *e* says /ē/ at the end of a syllable.
<u>e</u> lect	Underline /ē/; *e* says /ē/ at the end of a syllable.
<u>e</u> lec <u>ti</u>on	Underline /ē/; *e* says /ē/ at the end of a syllable.

wave   *A* says /ā/ because of the silent *e*; underline the silent *e* twice, and draw a bridge between the silent *e* and the *a*. English words do not end in v; underline the v.

lone ly   *O* says /ō/ because of the silent *e*; underline the silent *e* twice, and draw a bridge between the silent *e* and the *o*. Underline *y*. Vowel *y* says /ē/ at the end of a multi-syllable word.

blos soms

dare   *A* says /ā/ because of the silent *e*; underline the silent *e* twice, and draw a bridge between the silent *e* and the *a*.

steal

be sides²   *I* says /ī/ because of the silent *e*; underline the silent *e* twice, and draw a bridge between the silent *e* and the *i*.

tim id

bun ny   Underline *y*. Vowel *y* says /ē/ at the end of a multi-syllable word.

qu i et   Underline /ī/; *i* says /ī/ at the end of a syllable.

tracks   Phonogram *ck* is used only after a single vowel which says its first sound.

mes sag͡e̲̲   ***A*** says /ā/ because of the silent ***e***; underline the silent ***e*** twice, and draw a bridge between the silent ***e*** and the ***a***.

fr̲e̲e̲ze̲̲₅   Double underline the silent ***e***.

gal lon

es cap͡e̲̲   ***A*** says /ā/ because of the silent ***e***; underline the silent ***e*** twice, and draw a bridge between the silent ***e*** and the ***a***.

²
r̲e̲ sult   Underline /ē/; ***e*** says /ē/ at the end of a syllable.

A̲ mer i can   Underline /ā/; a says /ā/ at the end of a syllable.

vil lage̲   ***A*** says /ā/ because of the silent ***e***; underline the silent ***e*** twice, and draw a bridge between the silent ***e*** and the ***a***. ***G*** says /j/ because of the silent ***e***; underline the ***g***.

sa lute̲   ***U*** says /ū/ because of the silent ***e***; underline the silent ***e*** twice, and draw a bridge between the silent ***e*** and the ***u***.

sug gest   ***G*** may say /j/ before ***e***. Both letters ***g*** are sounded in this word. The first makes its hard sound, and the second makes its soft sound before the ***e***.

ac ci dent   ***C*** says /s/ before ***i***. Both letters ***c*** are sounded in this word. The first makes its hard sound, and the second makes its soft sound before the ***i***.

vol ume̲   ***U*** says /ū/ because of the silent ***e***; underline the silent ***e*** twice, and draw a bridge between the silent ***e*** and the ***u***.

pres i dents

torn

trench es

hats

pair

sh oes

broth er

coax

weight

196

fam i l<u>y</u>   Underline **y**. Vowel **y** says /ē/ at the end of a multi-syllable word.

r<u>ai</u>l r<u>oa</u>ds²   This is a compound word.

f<u>ur</u> ni tur͡<u>e</u>   **U** says /ū/ because of the silent **e**; underline the silent **e** twice, and draw a bridge between the silent **e** and the **u**.

ch͡ās<u>e</u>   **A** says /ā/ because of the silent **e**; underline the silent **e** twice, and draw a bridge between the silent **e** and the **a**.

fl<u>oa</u>t <u>ed</u>   Phonogram **ed** forms a new syllable when the base word ends in **d** or **t**.

cr<u>u</u> el   Underline /ū/; **u** says /ū/ at the end of a syllable.

<u>wreck</u>   Phonogram **ck** is used only after a single vowel which says its first sound.

trot <u>ted</u>   The base word is one syllable and ends in one vowel followed by one consonant, so we double the final consonant before adding a vowel suffix. Phonogram **ed** forms a new syllable when the base word ends in **d** or **t**.

cab in   hubs

s<u>oi</u>l   <u>sh</u>i v<u>er</u> ing

wag ons   com f<u>or</u>t

wit ness

curt sy — Underline **y**. Vowel **y** says /ē/ at the end of a multi-syllable word.

fife — **I** says /ī/ because of the silent **e**; underline the silent **e** twice, and draw a bridge between the silent **e** and the **i**.

2
u nit ed — When adding a vowel suffix, we drop the final silent **e** from the base word if it is no longer needed. Underline /ū/; **u** says /ū/ at the end of a syllable. Phonogram **ed** forms a new syllable when the base word ends in **d** or **t**.

states — **A** says /ā/ because of the silent **e**; underline the silent **e** twice, and draw a bridge between the silent **e** and the **a**.

sha dy — Underline /ā/; **a** says /ā/ at the end of a syllable. Underline **y**. Vowel **y** says /ē/ at the end of a multi-syllable word. When adding a vowel suffix, we drop the final silent **e** from the base word if it is no longer needed.

slice — **I** says /ī/ because of the silent **e**; underline the silent **e** twice, and draw a bridge between the silent **e** and the **i**. **C** says /s/ because of the silent **e**; underline the **c**.

hu man   Underline /ū/; **u** says /ū/ at the end of a syllable.

be side   Underline /ē/; **e** says /ē/ at the end of a syllable. **I** says /ī/ because of the silent **e**; underline the silent **e** twice, and draw a bridge between the silent **e** and the **i**.

por ch

3
stepped   The base word is one syllable and ends in one vowel followed by one consonant, so we double the final consonant before adding a vowel suffix.

ham

2
leaned

rob ber   The base word is one syllable and ends in one vowel followed by one consonant, so we double the final consonant before adding a vowel suffix.

sprang

man ner

dai² sie²s   Vowel **y** changes to **i** before adding any ending unless the ending begins with **i**.

la dy   Underline /ā/; **a** says /ā/ at the end of a syllable. Underline **y**. Vowel **y** says /ē/ at the end of a multi-syllable word.

plen ty   Underline **y**. Vowel **y** says /ē/ at the end of a multi-syllable word.

vi o lets   Underline /ī/; **i** says /ī/ at the end of a syllable. Underline /ō/; **o** says /ō/ at the end of a syllable.

tak² en   When adding a vowel suffix, we drop the final silent **e** from the base word if it is no longer needed. In this case, we drop the **e** and add **en**.

ma ³chine³₌5   Double underline the silent **e**.

dot   hun dred

shel ter² ed   beat en

storms²   tenth

scarf   num ber

gay

la<u>w</u>n

2
da<u>w</u>ns

<u>a</u> sid<u>e</u>   Underline /ā/; *a* says /ā/ at the end of a syllable. *A* says /ā/ because of the silent *e*; underline the silent *e* twice, and draw a bridge between the silent *e* and the *a*.

2
pray <u>er</u>s

put ti<u>n</u>g   The base word is one syllable and ends in one vowel followed by one consonant, so we double the final consonant before adding a vowel suffix.

x 3 2
<u>who</u>s<u>e</u>   *Wh* says /h/. Put a small X to show that it's an eXception.

2
p<u>o</u> si <u>ti</u>on   Underline /ō/; *o* says /ō/ at the end of a syllable.

bogs

3
slipp<u>ed</u>   The base word is one syllable and ends in one vowel followed by one consonant, so we double the final consonant before adding a vowel suffix.

2
stum bl<u>ed</u>   When adding a vowel suffix, we drop the final silent *e* from the base word if it is no longer needed; silent *e* provided the written vowel for the syllable.

point ing

dig

re turn   Underline /ē/; *e* says /ē/ at the end of a syllable.

be come₅   Double underline the silent *e*.

with out   This is a compound word.

cav̲e̲s [2] **A** says /ā/ because of the silent **e**; underline the silent **e** twice, and draw a bridge between the silent **e** and the **a**.

be̲ gins [2] Underline /ē/; **e** says /ē/ at the end of a syllable.

pranc̲e̲d [3] C says /s/ before **e**. When adding a vowel suffix, we drop the final silent **e** from the base word if it is no longer needed.

tast̲e̲ **A** says /ā/ because of the silent **e**; underline the silent **e** twice, and draw a bridge between the silent **e** and the **a**.

wh̲om [X 3] **Wh** says /h/. Put a small X to show that it's an eXception.

ma̲i̲d en

slen de̲r̲

pet als

a̲r̲ rest

pres ent [2]

god

ch̲ar i ot [3]

west e̲r̲n

le̲a̲ds [2]

neigh̲ e̲d̲ [2]

<u>sh</u>rill	We often double /l/ after a single vowel at the end of a base word.
sti<u>tch</u>	Phonogram *tch* is used only after a single vowel which does not say its name.

wr<u>in</u> kle<u>s</u> (2, =4) — Every syllable must have a written vowel; double underline the silent *e*.

<u>a</u> pron — Underline /ā/; *a* says /ā/ at the end of a syllable.

<u>a</u> pron ful (3) — Underline /ā/; *a* says /ā/ at the end of a syllable. When full is a suffix, it loses an *l*.

di<u>tch</u> — Phonogram *tch* is used only after a single vowel which does not say its name.

it self — This is a compound word.

sn<u>eez</u>ed (2) — When adding a vowel suffix, we drop the final silent *e* from the base word if it is no longer needed.

ham m<u>er</u>

tip t<u>oe</u>

l<u>ea</u> <u>th</u> er (2 2)

lap

sc<u>ar</u> let

st<u>oo</u>l (2)

d<u>ur</u> <u>ing</u>

this tle⁼⁼₄   Double underline the silent **t**. Every syllable must have a written vowel; double underline the silent **e**.

toad stool   This is a compound word.

fi nal   Underline /ī/; **i** says /ī/ at the end of a syllable.

ev er y thing   This is a compound word. Underline **y**. Vowel **y** says /ē/ at the end of a multi-syllable base word.

pos si ble⁼₄   Every syllable must have a written vowel; double underline the silent **e**.

de sire   Underline /ē/; **e** says /ē/ at the end of a syllable. **I** says /ī/ because of the silent **e**; underline the silent **e** twice, and draw a bridge between the silent **e** and the **i**.

suc cess   **C** says /s/ before **e**. Both letters **c** are sounded in this word. The first makes its hard sound, and the second makes its soft sound before the **e**. We often double /s/ after a single vowel at the end of a base word.

thick   Phonogram **ck** is used only after a single vowel which says its first sound.

um brel la³

sev er al

crept

stor²ed   When adding a vowel suffix, we drop the
            final silent **e** from the base word if it is no
            longer needed.

stem

hur ried   Vowel **y** changes to **i** before adding any ending
             unless the ending begins with **i**.

beets

un k<u>i</u>nd — Underline /ī/. **I** may say /ī/ when followed by two consonants.

fret f³ul — When full is a suffix, it loses an **l**.

hat<u>e</u> — **A** says /ā/ because of the silent **e**; underline the silent **e** twice, and draw a bridge between the silent **e** and the **a**.

<u>wr</u>app³<u>ed</u> — The base word is one syllable and ends in one vowel followed by one consonant, so we double the final consonant before adding a vowel suffix.

grap<u>e</u>s — **A** says /ā/ because of the silent **e**; underline the silent **e** twice, and draw a bridge between the silent **e** and the **a**.

str<u>aw</u> ber r²<u>ie</u>s — Vowel **y** changes to **i** before adding any ending unless the ending begins with **i**.

<u>au</u> tum<u>n</u> — Double underline the silent n.

b<u>e</u> tw<u>ee</u>n — Underline /ē/; **e** says /ē/ at the end of a syllable.

d<u>e</u> cíd<u>e</u> — Underline /ē/; **e** says /ē/ at the end of a syllable.

st<u>a</u> <u>ti</u>on — Underline /ā/; **a** says /ā/ at the end of a syllable.

hut — bun<u>ch</u>

cl<u>oa</u>k — won d<u>er</u>

pu<u>sh</u> ³<u>ed</u>

cent	C says /s/ before *e*.
cen t͟u ry	*C* says /s/ before *e*. Underline /ū/; *u* says /ū/ at the end of a syllable. Underline *y*. Vowel *y* says /ē/ at the end of a multi-syllable word.
b͟old	Underline /ō/. *O* may say /ō/ when followed by two consonants.
thron͟e	*O* says /ō/ because of the silent *e*; underline the silent *e* twice, and draw a bridge between the silent *e* and the *o*.
tun͟e	*U* says /ū/ because of the silent *e*; underline the silent *e* twice, and draw a bridge between the silent *e* and the *u*.
ti͟c͟k et	Phonogram *ck* is used only after a single vowel which says its first sound.
drill	We often double /l/ after a single vowel at the end of a base word.
stud y͟	Underline *y*. Vowel *y* says /ē/ at the end of a multi-syllable word.
w͟rit ten	When adding a vowel suffix, we drop the final silent *e* from the base word if it is no longer needed. In this case, we also double the final consonant which makes *i* say /ĭ/.

mer man   pearl

mer maid   ax

crown   crash

per sons

caw

lake

A says /ā/ because of the silent **e**; underline the
silent **e** twice, and draw a bridge between the
silent **e** and the **a**.

mile

I says /ī/ because of the silent **e**; underline the
silent **e** twice, and draw a bridge between the
silent **e** and the **i**.

en joy

par ty

Underline **y**. Vowel **y** says /ē/ at the end of a
multi-syllable word.

fa vor

Underline /ā/; **a** says /ā/ at the end of a syllable.

class

We often double /s/ after a single vowel at the
end of a base word.

wire

I says /ī/ because of the silent **e**; underline the
silent **e** twice, and draw a bridge between the
silent **e** and the **i**.

vote

O says /ō/ because of the silent **e**; underline
the silent **e** twice, and draw a bridge between the
silent **e** and the **o**.

chief

²
c<u>au</u>s<u>e</u>₌₅   Double underline the silent *e*.

sup p<u>or</u>t

t<u>er</u>m

   3 4
s<u>e</u> ri <u>ous</u>   Underline /ē/; *e* says /ē/ at the end of a syllable.

bean stalk — Double underline the silent *l*.

trea sures — *U* says /ū/ because of the silent *e*; underline the silent *e* twice, and draw a bridge between the silent *e* and the *u*.

nurse — Double underline the silent *e*.

joy ful — When full is a suffix, it loses an *l*.

pop u la tion — Underline /ū/; *u* says /ū/ at the end of a syllable. Underline /ā/; *a* says /ā/ at the end of a syllable.

pri vate — Underline /ī/; *i* says /ī/ at the end of a syllable. Double underline the silent *e*.

mu sic — Underline /ū/; *u* says /ū/ at the end of a syllable.

mar ket

silk

qu een

win

harp

thun der

fin ish ed

prac ti cal

mar r<u>y</u>   Underline **y**. Vowel **y** says /ē/ at the end of a multi-syllable word.

ques <u>ti</u>on   Think to spell /kwes-shon/.
Pronounce /kwes-chon./

li<u>e</u>   ***I*** says /ī/ because of the silent **e**; underline the silent **e** twice, and draw a bridge between the silent **e** and the **i**.

p<u>a</u> p<u>er</u>   Underline /ā/; **a** says /ā/ at the end of a syllable.

less   We often double /s/ after a single vowel at the end of a base word.

ton<u>gue</u>   Double underline the silent **u** and **e**. Some words have unusual spellings because of the language from which they came, or because of an old pronunciation, but "tongue" is just weird.

prop <u>er</u> t<u>y</u>   Underline **y**. Vowel **y** says /ē/ at the end of a multi-syllable word.

p<u>ur</u> pos<u>e</u>₅   Double underline the silent **e**.

<u>tai</u> <u>lor</u>   ink

<u>sh</u>op   c<u>ou</u>rt

fit   pub li<u>sh</u>

sud den

herd   Definition: a large group of animals.

$\overset{2}{\text{bo}}$oks

read   Homograph: $\overset{2}{\text{re}}$ad.

tend ing

flock   Phonogram **ck** is used only after a single vowel which says its first sound.

or der

sch ool

man age₃   **G** says /j/ because of the silent **e**; underline the **g**, and double underline the silent **e**.

whip

swung

press   We often double /s/ after a single vowel at the end of a base word.

drawn

re cov er   Underline /ē/; **e** says /ē/ at the end of a syllable.

sen ate₅   Double underline the silent **e**.

de vel op   Underline /ē/; **e** says /ē/ at the end of a syllable.

rain bow²   This is a compound word.

or ange₌₃   **G** says /j/ because of the silent **e**; underline the **g**, and double underline the silent **e**.

wipe   **I** says /ī/ because of the silent **e**; underline the silent **e** twice, and draw a bridge between the silent **e** and the **i**.

sun beams²   This is a compound word.

fif ty   Underline **y**. Vowel **y** says /ē/ at the end of a multi-syllable word.

wel come₌₅   Double underline the silent **e**.

ex am i na tion   Underline /ā/; **a** says /ā/ at the end of a syllable.

fa mous⁴   Underline /ā/; **a** says /ā/ at the end of a syllable.

for tune   **U** says /ū/ because of the silent **e**; underline the silent **e** twice, and draw a bridge between the silent **e** and the **u**.

fear

gowns²

wis dom²

light ning

rap id

crowds²

The next seven words are the days of the week. They are in order, so you'll be able to memorize them while you practice reading them. The names of the week are proper names, so each name begins with a capital letter.

Sun day

Mon day

Tu͡es² day   *U* says /ū/ because of the silent *e*; underline the silent *e* twice, and draw a bridge between the silent *e* and the *u*.

Wed nes² day   Think to spell Wed-nes-day.
Pronounce /wĕnz-dā/.

Thurs² day

Fri day   Underline /ī/; *i* says /ī/ at the end of a syllable.

Sat ur day

lots   hon or

be gun   in spect

spell   kn own²

ac tion   height²

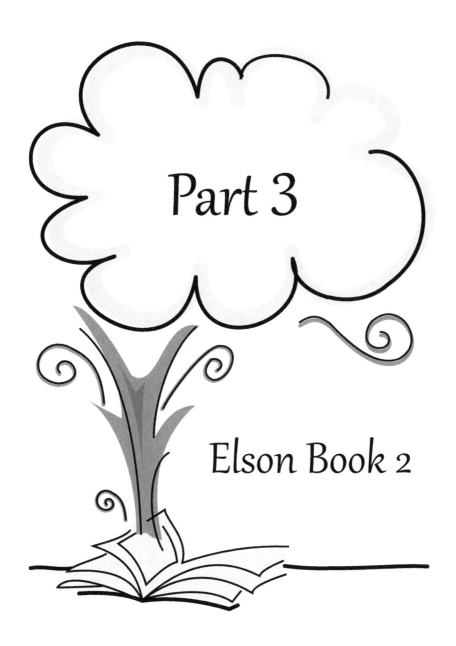

Part 3

Elson Book 2

We may see how all things are,
Seas and cities, near and far,
And the flying fairies' looks,
In the picture story-books.
Robert Louis Stevenson.

76. The Wake-Up Story

The sun was up. Five chicks and four geese and three rabbits and two kittens and one little dog were up, too.

They were all waiting for Baby Ray to come to the window. But Baby Ray was still fast asleep in his little white bed.

"Now I will get what he likes," said Mother. "When he wakes up, everything will be ready."

First she went along the garden path till she came to the old pump.

She said, "Good Pump, will you give me nice, clear water for the baby's bath?

The pump said, "I will."

The good old pump by the garden path
Gave nice, clear water for the baby's bath.

Then Mother went on till she came to the wood-pile.

She said, "Good Chips, the pump gave me nice, clear water for Baby Ray. Will you warm the water and cook the food?"

The chips said, "We will."

The good old pump by the garden path
Gave nice, clear water for the baby's bath.
And the big, white chips from the pile of wood
Were glad to warm it and to cook his food.

Mother went on till she came to the cow.

She said, "Good Cow, the pump gave me nice, clear water for Baby Ray. The wood- pile gave me big, white chips. Will you give me warm, rich milk?"

The cow said, "I will."

The good old pump by the garden path
Gave nice, clear water for the baby's bath.

And the big, white chips from the pile of wood
Were glad to warm it and to cook his food.
The cow gave milk in the milk-pail bright.

Top-knot Biddy was scratching in the ground.
Mother went to her and said, "Good Biddy, the pump gave me nice, clear water for Baby Ray. The wood-pile gave me big, white chips. The cow gave me warm, rich milk. Will you give me a new-laid egg?"
The hen said, "I will."

The good old pump by the garden path
Gave nice, clear water for the baby's bath.
And the big, white chips from the pile of wood
Were glad to warm it and to cook his food.
The cow gave milk in the milk-pail bright,
And Top-knot Biddy an egg new and white.

Then Mother went on till she came to the apple tree.
She said, "Good Tree, the pump gave me nice, clear water for Baby Ray. The wood- pile gave me big, white chips. The cow gave me warm, rich milk. The hen gave me a new-laid egg. Will you give me a pretty, red apple?
The tree said, "I will."

So Mother took the apple and the egg and the milk and the chips and the water to the house. There was Baby Ray looking out of the window!

Then she kissed him and bathed him and dressed him. While she was doing this she told him the Wake-Up Story:

> The good old pump by the garden path
> Gave nice, clear water for the baby's bath.
> And the big, white chips from the pile of wood
> Were glad to warm it and to cook his food.
> The cow gave milk in the milk-pail bright,
> And Top-knot Biddy an egg new and white.
> And the tree gave an apple so round and red,
> For dear Baby Ray who was just out of bed.

Eudora Bumstead, Adapted.

77. The Star Dipper

Once there was a little girl who was very, very kind. She and her mother lived in a little house. It was near a big woods.

One night her mother was sick. It was a very warm night.

"Oh, I am so thirsty," said her mother.

"I wish I had some nice, cool water."

"I will get you some water, Mother," said the little girl.

So she took an old tin dipper and ran to the pump. But the pump would not give her any water. The well was dry.

"What shall I do?" said the little girl. "My mother must have some nice, cool water. I will run to the spring in the woods. It is very dark, but I must not be afraid."

So she ran down the road to the dark woods. She could not see where she was going. The sharp stones cut her feet, but she ran on and on.

It was so dark that she lost her way among the trees. But she did not turn back. "I must get some water for my mother," she said.

At last she found the spring, and filled her dipper. Then she started back home.

On the way home she met a little dog. She knew that he must be thirsty, as all the brooks were dry.

"Come, little dog," said the kind girl. "I will give you some of this nice, cool water."

She poured some water into her hand, and the little dog drank and drank.

Then a queer thing happened. The old tin dipper turned to shining silver. It was as bright as the silver moon. Then the little girl could see her way.

She went on faster and faster. Soon she met an old, old man.

"Oh, I am so thirsty!" said the old man. "I have walked a long way. All the brooks are dry. Can you tell me where I can get a drink of nice, cool water?"

"I will give you some," said the little girl.

So she gave the old man a drink from her dipper. Then another queer thing happened.

The silver dipper turned to shining gold. It shone like the golden sun.

At last the little girl reached her home. She gave her mother the golden dipper. "Oh, how cool this water is!" said her mother. She drank and drank until there was no more water in the dipper.

"Thank you, my good little girl," said her mother. "I feel so much better now!"

Then a wonderful thing happened. The golden dipper turned to sparkling diamonds.

They went up, up, up into the sky and turned to seven bright stars. They made a star dipper in the sky.

That was a long, long time ago, but the star dipper is still in the sky. It shows how brave a kind-hearted little girl can be.

Old Tale.

78. Twinkle, Twinkle, Little Star

Twinkle, twinkle, little star;
   How I wonder what you are!
Up above the world so high,
   Like a diamond in the sky.

When the blazing sun is set,
   And the grass with dew is wet,
Then you show your little light,
   Twinkle, twinkle, all the night.

In the dark blue sky you keep,
   And often through my window peep;
For you never shut your eye
   Till the sun is in the sky.

And your bright and tiny spark
   Lights the traveler in the dark;

Though I know not what you are,
Twinkle, twinkle, little star.

Jane Taylor.

What Lights the Stars?

I've wondered, oh, so many times,
    What lights the stars at night,
And now, at last I've found it out!
    I know that I am right!

For only half an hour ago
    A band of bright fireflies
Danced in and out among the trees,
    A-searching for the skies!

And just a minute after that
    The stars shone clear and bright!
Of course, the fireflies lighted them!
    Now, tell me, am I right?

Emeline Goodrow.

79. The Naughty Shadow

Once there was a little boy who wanted his shadow to come to him. "Come to me!" the boy said. "I want you; come to me!"

But the shadow stood still.

Then the boy ran toward the shadow, but the shadow ran away. The little boy ran faster, but the shadow ran just as fast as he did. It would not come to him.

When at last the little boy was tired and sat down to rest, the shadow sat down, too.

"If you won't come to me," said the little boy, "sit still, and I will come to you."

The little boy got up, but the shadow got up, too.

Then the little boy became angry. "Do as you please," he said. "You are a naughty shadow. I shall not ask you again to come to me."

Then the little boy turned and ran away from the shadow. He ran and ran and ran.

After he had run a long time, he looked back.

There was the little shadow, close to him.

"Oho!" said the little boy. "Now I know how to make you come to me!"

Russian Tale.

80. My Shadow

I have a little shadow
    that goes in and out with me,
And what can be the use of him
    is more than I can see.
He is very, very like me
    from the heels up to the head.
And I see him jump before me,
    when I jump into my bed.

The funniest thing about him
    is the way he likes to grow—

Not at all like proper children,
  which is always very slow;
For he sometimes shoots up taller,
  like an India-rubber ball.
And he sometimes gets so little
  that there's none of him at all.

One morning, very early,
  before the sun was up,
I rose and found the shining dew
  on every buttercup;
But my lazy little shadow,
  like an arrant sleepy-head,
Had stayed at home behind me
  and was fast asleep in bed.

Robert Louis Stevenson.

Bed in Summer

In winter I get up at night,
And dress by yellow candle light;
In summer, quite the other way,
I have to go to bed by day.

I have to go to bed, and see
The birds still hopping on the tree,
Or hear the grown-up people's feet
Still going past me in the street.

And does it not seem hard to you,
When all the sky is clear and blue,
And I should like so much to play,
To have to go to bed by day?

Robert Louis Stevenson.

81. Lucky Hans

I

Hans had been away from home for seven years. He had worked hard, and now he wanted to go home to see his mother.

His master said to him, "You have been a good boy. You may go home, Hans. You have worked hard, and I will pay you well."

So he gave Hans a piece of silver as big as his head.

"How lucky I am!" said Hans. He tied up the silver in a big cloth and put it over his shoulder. Then he started for home.

It was a hot day, and the silver began to feel heavy. Hans soon got very tired.

By and by he saw a man coming down the road. He was riding on a fine horse.

The man was so happy that he sang a song as he rode along.

"Oh, dear!" said Hans. "How tired I am! This silver is so heavy that it hurts my shoulder. I wish I had a horse! Then I could be happy, too, and sing as I rode along. If I only had a fine horse!"

The mail heard Hans. "Why do you go on foot, then?" he asked.

"I go on foot because I have no horse," said Hans. "I have such a heavy load! It is only a piece of silver, but it is so heavy that it hurts my shoulder."

"Let us trade," said the man. "I will take the silver, and you may take the horse. When you want to go fast, pull the reins and say, 'Get up!'"

"I shall be glad to trade," said Hans.

So the man took the silver, and Hans got on the horse. "How lucky I am!" he said.

Away he rode on his horse.

Soon he wanted to go faster. He pulled the reins and said, "Get up!" Away went the horse, faster and faster. Away went Hans, too, off the horse. The horse ran away as fast as he could go.

II

Just then another man came along. This man was driving a cow. He caught the horse and brought it back to Hans.

"How do you feel?" asked the man.

"Oh, I had a hard fall," said Hans. "No more horses for me! I wish I had your cow. I could walk slowly after her along the sunny road. I could have nice, rich milk every day."

"Let us trade," said the man. "You take the cow, and I will take the horse."

"I shall be glad to trade," said Hans.

Hans clapped his hands for joy. "How lucky I am!" he said.

The man got on the horse and rode away.

Hans drove the cow slowly along the road. He walked on and on and on until he got very tired.

He got thirsty, too, oh, so thirsty! "I know what to do," said Hans. "I will milk my cow and drink the milk."

So he tied the cow to a tree. Then he tried to milk her, but he could not get a drop of milk.

He tried and tried until the cow got very cross. At last she kicked Hans, and over he went in the dust.

Hans lay on the ground a long time. At last a butcher came along the road. He had a pig in a wheelbarrow.

"What happened to you, my boy?" asked the man. Hans told him. "That cow will give no milk," said the butcher. "She is an old cow. She must be killed for beef."

"Oh, dear!" said Hans. "I don't like beef. I wish I had a pig. Then I could kill it and eat it. I like pork better."

"Let us trade," said the butcher. "You take the pig, and I will take the cow."

"How lucky I am!" said Hans. He gave the cow to the butcher. Then he took the pig, and tied a string around its leg.

Off he went, driving the pig. "Now my troubles are over," he said.

By and by he met a man carrying a goose.

"Where are you going?" asked the man.

Hans told him about the horse and the cow. "Now I have a fine pig," said Hans.

The man shook his head. "I am sorry for you, my boy," he said. "Your pig may get you into trouble. Do you see that little town over there? It is on your way.

"A pig has been stolen there and they are looking for the thief. They will see this pig and will think it is the stolen pig. Then they will throw you into the pond."

This frightened Hans very much. "Let us trade," he said. "You take the pig, and I will take the goose."

"Very well," said the man. So they made the trade.

"How lucky I am to get rid of that pig!" said Hans, as he walked along, carrying the big white goose.

III

When he got to the little town, he saw a scissors-grinder working and singing.

"You look happy," said Hans.

"I am happy," said the man. "A good scissors-grinder always has money in his pocket. Where did you buy that fine goose?"

"I did not buy it," said Hans. "I traded a pig for it."

"Where did you buy the pig?" asked the scissors-grinder.

"I did not buy it, either," answered Hans. "I traded a cow for it."

"Where did you get the cow?" asked the scissors-grinder.

"I traded a horse for it," answered Hans.

"Where did you get the horse?" asked the scissors-grinder.

"I traded a piece of silver for the horse," answered Hans. "The piece of silver was too heavy for me to carry."

"Where did you get the silver?" asked the scissors-grinder.

"Oh, I worked seven long years for that," answered Hans.

"You have done well," said the scissors- grinder, "but you can do better. You can always find money in your pocket."

"How can I do that?" asked Hans.

"You must be a scissors-grinder," said the man. "All you need is a grindstone."

"Let us trade," said Hans. "You take the goose, and I will take the grindstone."

"I am willing," said the scissors-grinder.

So they made the trade.

"How lucky I am!" said Hans as the scissors-grinder went off with the goose.

Hans took the grindstone and walked on and on and on until he got very tired.

By and by he came to a pond. "How thirsty I am!" said Hans. He put the grind- stone on the bank and stooped down to get a drink.

Just then the grindstone fell over, and into the pond it went.

Hans watched it go down, down into the water until he could see it no longer. Now he had no grindstone to carry.

Hans was as happy as he could be. "How lucky I am!" he said. "No one was ever so lucky as I."

Then he went on to his mother's house.

Old Tale.

82. The Lost Doll

I once had a sweet little doll, dears,
    The prettiest doll in the world;
Her cheeks were so red and so white, dears,
    And her hair was so charmingly curled.

But I lost my poor little doll, dears,
    As I played on the heath one day;
And I cried for her more than a week, dears,
    But I never could find where she lay.

I found my poor little doll, dears,
    As I played on the heath one day;

Folks say she is terribly changed, dears,
　　For her paint is all washed away.

And her arm's trodden off by the cows, dears,
　　And her hair's not the least bit curled;
Yet for old sakes' sake, she is still, dears,
　　The prettiest doll in the world.

Charles Kingsley.

83. The Ant and the Grasshopper

Once an ant and a grasshopper lived in the same field.

The ant was a great worker. In summer she laid up food for the winter. But the grasshopper was lazy and played all day.

"Why do you work so hard, friend ant?" said the grasshopper, one summer day. "I dance and sing and have a good time."

"If I play in summer," said the ant, "what shall I do for food in winter?"

"Winter is a long way off," said the grasshopper, as he went away, singing.

"Poor grasshopper!" said the ant. "He will live and learn."

At last winter came. The birds had all gone away, and snow covered the ground.

How cold it was!

The ant had gone into her warm house, which was full of food. The cold could not harm her. But the poor grasshopper had no home and no food. He was stiff with cold, and he was very hungry, too.

So the grasshopper went to the ant's house.

"Will you give me something to eat?" he asked. "I have had nothing to eat for two days. The snow is so deep that I can find no food."

"Poor grasshopper!" said the ant. "In summer you sang while I was hard at work. Now you may dance for your supper."

Retold from a Fable by Aesop.

84. The Foolish Frog

Once an ox came to a pond to get a drink of water. Some little frogs were playing on the bank of the pond. They had never seen an ox before, and they were very much frightened.

So they ran to their mother and said, "Oh, Mother, we have seen such a big animal, drinking all the water out of our pond!"

Now, the mother was a proud old frog who thought that she could puff herself up and make herself as big as the strange animal was.

"How big was this wonderful beast that you saw? Was it as big as this?" she asked, blowing and puffing herself out.

"Oh, it was much bigger than that, Mother," said the young frogs.

Then puffing and blowing with all her might, she asked them, "Was this strange animal as big as I am now?"

"Oh, Mother," answered the little frogs, "if you were to try till you burst, you would not be half as big as the beast that we saw drinking in the pond."

The silly old frog was so proud that she tried again and again to puff herself out still more.

But each time the little frogs told her that the strange beast was bigger than she was. At last she puffed so hard that she burst herself.

How foolish it is to try to do something that we cannot do.

Retold from a Fable by Aesop.

85. Pleasing Everybody

Once an old man and his little boy were taking a small donkey to the next town, where they wanted to sell it. They walked along the road together and drove the donkey before them.

On the way they met a man who said to them, "How foolish you are! Surely that donkey is stronger than you are. Why does not one of you get on his back and ride? Riding is easier than walking."

So the old man put the boy on the donkey's back, and they went on again.

Soon they met another man. "You lazy boy!" he cried. "Are you not ashamed to ride, and let your poor old father go along the road on foot?"

So the old man told the little boy to get off and walk. Then the old man got on the donkey's back, and they went on again, toward the town.

Then two women came along. One of them said, "Look at that selfish old man. He rides, and makes his poor little boy walk. There is room enough on the donkey's back for both the old man and the little boy."

So the old man told the boy to sit on the donkey's back behind him, and they rode along together.

Soon they met another man, who asked them, "Is that your own donkey?"

"It is," answered the old man.

"I should not think so," said the man.

"If it is your donkey, why do you give it such a heavy load? You two are better able to carry that poor little donkey than he is to carry you."

So the old man and the little boy got off the donkey and tied its legs to a pole. Then they put the pole over their shoulders, and in this way carried the donkey.

The load was so very heavy that they had to walk slowly.

By and by they reached the town. "Ho, ho! Ho, ho, ho!" laughed every one they met.

"What a funny sight! Who ever saw a man and a boy carrying a donkey? Ho, ho! Ho!"

The old man became very angry. He put the donkey down, untied him, and threw away the pole.

"Now I shall do just what I thought best at first," he said to the little boy. "You and I will walk, and we will drive the donkey before us."

He who tries to please everybody pleases nobody.

Retold from a Fable by Aesop.

86. The Dog in the Manger

A dog once lay in a manger that was full of hay.

A hungry ox came to the manger and wanted to eat the hay, but the dog barked at him and would not let him have any of it.

"You selfish old dog!" said the ox. "You ought to be made to starve the rest of your life. For you cannot eat the hay, and you will not let anyone else have any."

Retold from a Fable by Aesop.

87. Little Mouse and the Strangers

Little Mouse: Squeak! Squeak! Squeak! Oh, Mother, Mother! I have had such a fright!

Mother Mouse: What has happened, Little Mouse? Where have you been?

Little Mouse: Oh, Mother! I was tired of our little home, so I have been out to see the world.

Mother Mouse: Oh, my dear child! Did you go all alone? No wonder you are frightened. Home is best for Little Mouse. Where did you go?

Little Mouse: I went to the barnyard. Squeak! Squeak! It frightens me yet, when I think of it.

Mother Mouse: Tell me about it. What did you see to frighten you so?

Little Mouse: At first I was not frightened. I saw a beautiful animal who looked a little like me.

Mother Mouse: A little like you? Oh, no! There is no one like you in the barnyard.

Little Mouse: Yes, she was like me, Mother, but she was much bigger than I am. She had fur like mine, but it was much longer.

Mother Mouse: Little Mouse, you frighten me. Quick, quick! Tell me more about this animal. I am afraid I know who it was.

Little Mouse: She was lying on the grass, in the sun. She looked kind and gentle. I thought she might like little mice, so I started to go up and speak to her. She made a pleasant sound—purr-r, purr-r, purr-r!

Mother Mouse: Oh, my dear Little Mouse, that was a cat! You have been in great danger. The cat does like little mice, but she likes them to eat! Quick, tell me! You did not try to speak to her, did you?

Little Mouse: No, Mother. I did not have time. For just then I saw a strange and dreadful animal.

Mother Mouse: Who could that be. Little Mouse? The cat is the most dreadful animal you could see.

Little Mouse: Oh, no, Mother! Listen, and I will tell you. This animal had a long, sharp nose.

Mother Mouse: A long, sharp nose? The pig has a long nose, but it is not sharp.

Little Mouse: He had a red chin that shook when he moved.

Mother Mouse: A red chin? None of the animals in the barnyard has a red chin. This must have been a strange, wild beast. Tell me more about him.

Little Mouse: He had something red on his head, too, and he had only two legs. He stretched out his long neck and made a dreadful noise—Cock-a-doodle-doo! Cock-a-doodle-doo!

Mother Mouse: Oh, squee-hee-hee! Never mind if I laugh, Little Mouse. Now I know what the strange beast was. That was a rooster! He has a red comb and a long beak, but he will not harm you.

Little Mouse: But, Mother, how shall I tell what beasts will harm me? The cat looked so kind, and the rooster looked so fierce.

Mother Mouse: Do not speak to strange beasts. You cannot tell by their looks what they will do. Remember, Little Mouse, that good deeds are better than good looks.

Retold from a Fable by Aesop.

88. The Cow

The friendly cow, all red and white,
    I love with all my heart;
She gives me cream with all her might
    To eat with apple-tart.

She wanders, lowing, here and there,
    And yet she cannot stray,
All in the pleasant open air,
    The pleasant light of day.

And blown by all the winds that pass,
    And wet with all the showers,
She walks among the meadow grass
    And eats the meadow flowers.

Robert Louis Stevenson.

89. Taro and the Turtle

Taro was a fisherman who lived long, long ago. He was young and strong, and he could catch more fish than anybody else.

He was very kind, too. In all his life he never had teased or hurt anything.

One time when Taro had been fishing all day, he was very tired and hung-ry. He was going home to eat and rest.

On his way he saw some boys who had caught a turtle and were teasing it.

Taro felt so sorry for the turtle that he gave the boys some money, and they gave him the turtle. Then

Taro talked kindly to the boys until they promised him not to tease animals again.

Taro stroked the turtle's back. "Poor thing!" he said. "I will take you to your home in the sea. I have heard that a turtle can live a thousand years. Do not let anyone catch you again. Then you will live a thousand years."

So Taro put the turtle into the water and went home, for he was tired.

The next morning Taro got up early and went out in his boat to fish. The sky and the sea were very blue, and the air was soft and warm.

Taro went on and on in his little boat.

He passed all the other boats and went far, far out on the sea.

"Oh, I am so happy!" he said. "I wish I could live a thousand years, like the turtle."

All at once Taro heard someone calling him. "Taro! Taro! Taro!" called the voice.

The voice was as clear as a bell.

Taro stood up in his boat and looked out over the water, but he could see no boats.

"Who is calling me?" he asked.

"I am calling you, Taro," said a clear, soft voice. "I have come to thank you for saving my life."

There, by the side of the boat, was the turtle that Taro had put back into the water.

"Will you come with me, Taro?" said the turtle. "I will take you to my home. It is in the Sea-King's palace at the bottom of the sea. It is always summer there."

"I am strong," said Taro, "but I cannot swim so far."

"Get on my back," said the turtle.

"Oh, you are too small," said Taro. "You cannot carry me. I am very sorry that I cannot go. I should like to see the Sea-King's palace, and the land of summer."

Taro looked sadly at the turtle. But what did he see? The turtle was getting bigger and bigger! It grew bigger than Taro!

"Now I am not too small," said the turtle.

Taro got on its back. Down they went into the sea, through the clear water.

At last they saw a great gate and behind it the Sea-King's palace. All around it was the land of summer, where birds sang and flowers bloomed.

Taro and the turtle went up to the great gate. A gatekeeper stood there. He was a fish, and all his helpers were fishes.

"This is Taro," said the turtle. Then all at once the turtle was gone.

"Come with us, Taro," said the gatekeeper. "We know where to take you."

The gate opened, and Taro and the fishes went into the Sea-King's palace.

They took him to a beautiful Princess.

Her dress was green, like the water, and her voice was as clear as a bell.

"Come here, Taro," she said. "I am the Sea-King's child. Yesterday you saved my life. Here in the land of summer I am a Princess. When I go to your land I change to a turtle. I was the turtle you saved.

"This morning I heard you wish you could live a thousand years. Come and live with me. I will share everything with you."

So Taro and the Princess lived a thousand years in the land of summer, under the sea.

Japanese Tale.

90. The Elephant and the Monkey

Once upon a time an elephant and a monkey had a quarrel.

The elephant was proud because he was so strong. "See how big and strong I am!" he said. "Can you pull a tree down?"

Now the monkey was proud because he was so quick. "See how fast I can run and climb!" he said. "Can you climb a tree? Can you hang by your tail from a branch?"

At last they went to a wise old owl.

"We cannot agree," they said. "Tell us what you think about it. Which is better—to be strong, or to be quick?"

The owl said to them, "Do just as I tell you, so that I may find out which is better. Do you see that great fruit tree across the river? Go and pick the fruit and bring it to me."

So they went to the river, but the water was so swift that the monkey was afraid.

"Get on my back," said the elephant, proudly. "I am big and strong. I am not afraid to swim across a swift river."

So the monkey got on the elephant's back, and they soon got across the river.

On they went until they came to the tree.

It was so tall that the fruit hung high above them.

The elephant tried to break the tree down, but it was too strong. He tried to reach the fruit with his trunk, but it was too high.

"Wait a minute," said the monkey, proudly. "I can climb." He ran quickly up the tree, and threw down the rich, ripe fruit.

The elephant put it into his great mouth.

Then they crossed the stream, and gave the fruit to the owl.

"Now," they said, "which is better—to be strong, or to be quick?"

"Can anyone tell which is better?" asked the owl. "Neither of you could get the fruit alone.

"It took the elephant's strength and the monkey's quickness. One crossed the stream; the other gathered the fruit."

A Tale from India.

91. The Bear Who Played Soldier

Once a man had a tame bear which he took from place to place. The bear could march and play ball and dance.

Children came to see the man and his tame bear. They gave money to see the bear dance.

The bear was so big and black that he looked very fierce. But he really was kind and gentle.

One night the man went to an inn to eat his supper. He thought that the bear was tied fast to a tree outside.

The inn-keeper had three little boys. The oldest was six years old, the next was four, and the baby was two.

The little boys were upstairs playing soldier. Each one had a gun, and the oldest boy had a drum. They marched round and round. The oldest boy beat the drum. They were having a fine time.

Then they heard a noise—tramp, tramp! Tramp, tramp! Tramp, tramp! Someone was coming upstairs. Who was it? The door opened, and the big black bear came in.

The children were so frightened that they hid in corners of the room. The big bear went to each one. He snuffed at them, but he did not hurt them.

By and by the children came out of the corners and said, "This is only a big black dog."

They began to pat the bear, and then he lay down, and the baby climbed on him.

Soon the oldest boy got his drum again and began to beat it—rat-a-tat-tat! Rat-a-tat- tat! Rat-a-tat-too!

The bear got up on his hind legs and began to dance. "The big dog wants to play soldier," said the children. "Let us play."

So the children got their guns. The bear wanted a gun, too, so they gave him one. He knew how to hold it just right.

Then the children began to march around the room with the bear. Left, right! Left, right! Rat-a-tat-tat! Rat-a-tat-too!

Just then the mother of the children came in and saw the big bear. Oh, how frightened she was! She called for help, and the bear's master came running up the stairs.

"Do not be afraid of my bear," he said.

"He is tame and will not hurt the children."

Then he led the bear away.

"We like to play soldier with the big dog," said the baby. "Let him come again."

Hans Christian Andersen.

92. The New Voices

Once the birds and the beasts all grew tired of their voices.

The fox said, "I want to crow like the rooster." The hawk said, "I want to chirp like the sparrow." The wolf said, "I want to bleat like the sheep."

Every bird and every animal in the world wanted to change.

So they went to the Wise Man. "We are all tired of our voices," they said. "We want to change them. You are wise and know how to teach us. Will you help us to get our wish?"

"I will teach you," said the Wise Man.

"But you must make good use of your new voices."

So he taught each bird and each animal how to change his voice. They all went back to their homes as happy as they could be.

Soon afterwards, the fox went to the barnyard. "Cock-a-doodle-doo! Cock-a-doodle-doo!" he called. "See this fat worm. Come and get it! Come and get it!"

When the hens heard him, they thought it was the rooster. They ran to get the worm, and the fox ate them up.

Then the wolf went to the sheep fold.

"Baa-baa! Baa-baa!" he called. "It is late, and I am tired. Open the door, my little lambs, and let me come in. Please do not keep me waiting."

The lambs heard him. "That is mother," they said, as they ran to open the door.

Then the wolf ate them up.

The hawk went to the sparrows' nest. "Tweet-tweet! Tweet-tweet!" he called. He tapped on the side of the nest.

"That is father," said the little sparrows.

"He has something nice for breakfast." As soon as they put out their heads, the hawk ate them up.

Soon many beasts and birds began to do harm to each other.

Then the Wise Man was sorry that he had taught them how to get new voices. So he called them together and said, "This will never do. You must take back your own voices, because you have not made good use of your new ones.

"Everything you learn should help you to do good."

A Tale from India.

93. The Swallow

Fly away, fly away, over the sea,
 Sun-loving swallow, for summer is done;
Come again, come again, come back to me,
 Bringing the summer and bringing the sun.

When you come hurrying home over the sea,
 Then we are certain that winter is past;
Cloudy and cold though your pathway may be,
 Summer and sunshine will follow you fast.

Fly away, fly away, over the sea,
 Sun-loving swallow, for summer is done;
Come again, come again, come back to me,
 Bringing the summer and bringing the sun.

Christina G. Rossetti.

94. The Old Woman Who Wanted All the Cakes

One day an old woman was baking cakes. She wore a black dress and a little white cape. On her head was a little red cap.

A poor old man said to her, "I am hungry. Please give me one of those nice cakes."

The little old woman said, "I will bake you one little cake. That is all you may have."

So she took a small piece of dough. She rolled it and rolled it. Then she patted it and patted it, and made a small cake.

But it began to grow bigger and bigger. "I will not give you this cake," said the old woman. "It is too big." So she put it into the oven for herself.

Then she took a tiny bit of dough. She rolled it and rolled it. Then she patted it and patted it, and made a tiny cake.

But it began to grow bigger and bigger.

"I will not give you this cake," said the old woman. "It is much too big." So she put that cake into the oven for herself, too.

Then she tried again with a tiny, tiny bit of dough, as small as a grain of wheat.

She rolled it and patted it and made a cake as small as a grain of wheat.

But that cake began to grow, too. It got bigger and bigger and bigger.

"I will not give you any cake at all," said the old woman. "These cakes are all too big to give away. I want them myself."

So the old man went away, hungry, and the old woman sat down to eat the cakes.

As she was eating, she began to grow smaller. She got smaller and smaller.

She felt her nose—it was a beak! She looked at her hands—they were wings! She looked at her feet—they were claws!

She still had on a black dress and a white cape and a little red cap. But they were all feathers! She had changed to a bird.

You will see the little old woman some day. She hops up and down trees, hunting for food. She has to work hard to get it.

You will know her when you see her. You will say, "There is the black dress, and the white cape, and the little red cap."

For the old woman was changed to a woodpecker.

Norse Tale.

95. Robin's Secret

We have a secret, just we three,
The robin and I and the sweet cherry tree;
The bird told the tree, and the tree told me,
And nobody knows it but just us three.

But of course the robin knows it best,
Because it built the—I shan't tell the rest;
And laid the four little—somethings—in it—
I am afraid I shall tell it every minute.

But if the tree and the robin don't peep,

I'll try my best the secret to keep;

Though I know when the little birds fly about,

Then the whole secret will be out.

96. Little Bird Blue

Little Bird Blue, come sing us your song;
The cold winter weather has lasted so long,
We're tired of skates, and we're tired of sleds,
We're tired of snow-banks as high as our heads;
    Now we're watching for you,
    Little Bird Blue.

Soon as you sing, then the springtime will come;
The robins will call and the honey-   bees hum,
And the dear little kitties, so cunning and gray,
Will sit in the willow-trees over the way;
    So hurry; please do,
    Little Bird Blue!

97. The Magpie's Lesson

One spring all the birds wanted to build their nests. "The magpie knows how," they said. "Let us ask her to show us. She makes the best nest."

"Yes, come and watch me," said the magpie. "See! First I take some mud. Then I shape it like a cup."

"Oh, I see how to do it!" said the thrush.

Away she flew to build her nest. So all thrushes have a nest like a mud-cup.

"Next I get some sticks," said the magpie. "I lay them in the mud."

"Now I know all about it," said the blackbird. Away she flew to build her nest. So the blackbird's nest is nothing but mud and sticks.

"Then I take some twigs," said the magpie. "I wind them around the nest."

"That is a fine plan," said the sparrow.

Away she flew to build her nest. So the sparrows always make a rough nest of twigs.

"Now I take soft feathers to make a lining for the nest," said the magpie.

"That suits me," said the swallow. Away she flew to build her nest. So the swallows all have warm nests lined with soft feathers.

"Last, I take more mud and sticks," said the magpie, "to build the nest higher."

But none of the birds heard her. They had all gone to build their nests.

So that is why the nests of birds are not alike.

The magpie's nest is still the best of all.

Old English Tale.

98. The Little Rabbit Who Wanted Red Wings

Once a little white rabbit lived in a warm hole at the foot of an old tree. He had everything a little rabbit could need, but he was always wishing for something more.

One day when Bobbie Squirrel went by, White Rabbit said to his mother, "Oh, I wish I had a tail like Bobbie Squirrel's!"

When Mr. Porcupine went by, he said, "Oh, I wish I had needles on my back like Mr. Porcupine's!"

When Mrs. Duck went by, he said, "Oh, I wish I had feathers like Mrs. Duck's!"

His mother grew very tired of hearing him always wishing for something.

One day old Mr. Ground Hog came by and heard White Rabbit saying, "I wish, I wish, I wish."

"Why don't you go down to the Wishing Pond?" said old Mr. Ground Hog. "If you look at yourself in the water and then turn around three times, you will get what you wish for."

Without even saying good-bye to his mother, White Rabbit hopped away to look for the Wishing Pond. He hopped and hopped, until at last he found it in the cool green woods.

There he saw a little red bird sitting by the Pond, drinking some water.

As soon as White Rabbit saw the bird he began to wish again. "Oh, I wish I had red wings!" he said. Just then he looked in the Wishing Pond, and saw himself in the water.

Then he turned around three times, and something queer happened. Two long red wings grew out from his shoulders!

He started at once for home to show them to his mother. But when he reached his home it was nearly dark, and the door was tight shut.

He knocked at the door, and his mother peeped out and saw him, but she would not let him come in. She did not know him, for she had never before seen a rabbit with red wings. So he had to look for some other place to sleep.

He went to many animal holes, but no one would let him come in. Nobody wanted such a queer-looking rabbit in his house.

At last he went to old Mr. Ground Hog's house. Mr. Ground Hog knew him at once, and let him come in. White Rabbit slept on the hard floor that night. It was not at all like his own soft, warm bed.

In the morning old Mr. Ground Hog said, "Don't you like red wings, White Rabbit?"

"No, no, no!" said little White Rabbit. "Well," said old Mr. Ground Hog, "why don't you go to the Wishing Pond, and wish them off again?"

Away went White Rabbit to the Wishing Pond as fast as he could hop. He made a wish, and looked at himself in the water. He turned around three times, and off went his red wings.

How happy he was! He hopped home to his mother like the wind. She knew him this time, and let him come in at once.

White Rabbit was so happy that he never again wished for anything he did not have.

From For the Story Teller by Carolyn S. Bailey.

99. The Animals That Found a Home

I

Once upon a time there was a ram that was being fed so that he would become fat.

One day when the man brought him food he said, "Eat all you want, poor ram. You will not be here long. Soon you will be mutton."

"I think I shall have something to say about that," said the ram. "I would rather be ram than mutton."

So he ate all the food he could. Then he put his head down and ran against the door. He struck it with his horns, and it flew open.

"Now I am free!" said the ram. "I will find my friend, the pig."

The pig was in the pen, eating from a pail full of corn. He looked very fat.

"Good-day, and thanks for your kindness last time we met," said the ram to the pig.

"Good-day, and thanks to you," said the pig. "I am very glad to see you."

"Do you know why they feed you so well?" asked the ram.

"No," said the pig. "Can you tell me?"

"Well, eat all you want now, poor pig. You will not be here long. Soon you will be pork," said the ram.

"I think I shall have something to say about that," said the pig. "I would rather be pig than pork."

"Then come with me," said the ram. "We will go to the woods and build a house, and live by ourselves."

"Very well," said the pig. "This is a good time to start."

When they had gone a little way, they met a goose. The goose was very fat, too. She was eating meal as fast as she could.

"Good-day, and thanks for your kindness last time we met," said the ram.

"Good-day, and thanks to you," said the goose.

"Do you know why they feed you so well?" asked the ram.

"No," said the goose. "Can you tell me?"

"Well, eat all you want now, poor goose. Soon you will he a roasted goose."

"I think I shall have something to say about that," said the goose. "I would rather be a live goose than a roasted goose. Where are you going?"

"We are going to the woods to build a house," said the ram.

"Let me go with you. I will help you," said the goose.

"Gabbling and quacking will not build a house," said the pig. "What can you do?"

"I can gather moss and fill the cracks," said the goose.

"Well, you may come with us," said the pig. "I like to be warm."

When they had gone a little farther, they saw a rooster. He was eating grain.

"Good-day, and thanks for your kindness last time we met," said the ram.

"Good-day, and thanks to you," said the rooster.

"Do you know why they feed you so well?" asked the ram.

"No," said the rooster. "Can you tell me?"

"Well, eat all you want now, poor rooster. Soon you will be soup."

"I think I shall have something to say about that," said the rooster. "I would rather be a rooster than soup. Where are you and the pig and the goose going?"

"We are going to the woods to build a house," said the ram.

"May I go with you?" said the rooster. "I will help you to build your house."

"Flapping and crowing will not build a house," said the pig. "What can you do?"

"I am early to rise and early to crow," said the rooster. "I can wake you early in the morning."

"You may go with us," said the pig. "It is hard for me to wake up. You may come and crow for us.

"Early to rise.

Makes you wealthy and wise."

II

So they all set off to the woods together and built the house.

The ram and the pig were strong. They did the hard work. The goose gathered moss and filled the cracks. The rooster crowed to get them up early.

Soon the house was ready. The roof was covered with bark, and they had a snug little home. They were very happy together.

Two hungry wolves lived in the woods near by. When they first saw the little house, one of them said, "We have neighbors. I wonder what they are like."

"I will go to see," said the other. "Maybe I can get some breakfast." He went to the little house, opened the door, and walked in.

Now the ram and his friends had been expecting the wolf. They knew what kind of breakfast he liked.

As soon as he came in, the ram ran against him and struck him with his strong horns.

The pig snapped and bit. The goose nipped and pecked. The rooster flew up to the house-top and crowed.

They threw the wolf out of the house. He ran back to his home as fast as he could go.

"How do you like our new neighbors?" asked the other wolf.

"Our neighbors!" cried the wolf. "Nice neighbors they are! A great giant came and struck me with his head.

"Then a troll tried to eat me up, while a witch with scissors snipped off bits of my toes, and someone on the roof called out, 'Throw him up to me! Throw him up to me!' You may be sure that I will never go to that house again."

So the wolves kept away, and the ram and his friends were happy in the little home, and ate all they wanted.

"Now we can get as fat as we please," said the pig.

Old Norse Tale.

100. The Bell of Atri

I

Good King John lived in Atri long ago. He wished everyone to be happy. He was sorry when anyone did wrong.

One day he said, "I have a plan that will help my people. I will build a tower with a bell in it. The bell-rope shall be so long that anyone can reach it. Even little children can ring the bell.

"When anyone is in trouble he may go to the bell-tower and ring the bell. Then one of my judges must go to the bell-tower, too. He must hear what the one who rings the bell has to say.

"The judge will find out why the man is in trouble. He will learn who has harmed the man. Then he must punish the one who did wrong.

"This will teach my people to do good. They will try to be kind to each other. They will try to do no wrong to anyone."

So good King John built a great bell- tower. The bell-rope was so long that even a child could reach it. All the people thought it was a fine plan.

When anyone was in trouble he went to the great bell-tower and rang the bell.

Then the judge put on his rich robes and ran to the bell-tower. He heard what the man had to say, and found the one who had done wrong. If he thought best, he punished him.

The bell hung in the tower many years. It was rung so often that at last the rope grew thin. Then someone tied a piece of hay around it to make it stronger.

One summer day the sun shone brightly on the bell-tower. It was very hot in Atri, and all the people were indoors. Everyone was taking a rest.

All at once the bell rang. "Ding-dong! I tell of wrong! Ding-dong! I tell of wrong!" it called.

The judge woke from his nap. "Some wrong has been done," he said. "I must see who is in trouble."

He put on his rich robes and went quickly to the tower. All the people ran to see who had rung the bell.

When they got to the tower—what do you think they saw?

A poor old horse was ringing the bell!

He was eating the piece of hay that was tied around the bell-rope. As he ate the hay, he pulled the rope. Then the bell rang, loud and clear—"Ding-dong! I tell of wrong!"

II

At first the judge was very angry. "I have lost my nap," he said. "I came here as fast as I could to see what poor man was in trouble. But I find only a hungry horse eating the bell-rope.

"Who put that piece of hay on the rope? Find the man who did it, and bring him to me. Take this horse away. What right has he to be here?"

Then the judge looked again at the horse. The poor beast was lame and almost blind. The judge saw that he was very thin. He knew that someone had done a wrong to the poor old horse.

"This poor horse is very hungry," said the judge. "He is almost starving. That is why he is so thin.

That is why he is eating the piece of hay. Who owns this horse?"

An old man answered him.

"This horse belongs to a rich man," he said. "See, he lives in that beautiful castle. This horse carried him when he went to war. More than once this horse has saved his master's life.

"But when the horse got too old to work, his master turned him out. Now the poor old beast goes around and picks up his food wherever he can get it.

"He has nothing to eat unless he finds it for himself, and so he is hungry almost all the time."

The judge was very angry when he heard that such a brave horse had a bad master.

"This poor horse is in trouble," he said. "He did well to ring King John's bell. Bring his master to me."

So the master was brought to the judge.

"Why have you left this poor horse to starve?" said the judge. "Did he not work for you as long as he could? Did he not save your life many times?"

The master hung his head in shame. He had not a word to say.

"You must care for this poor beast as long as he lives," said the judge. "You must let him go back to his stable, and you must give him all the food he needs."

All the people clapped their hands.

"The poor horse will never be hungry again," they said. "How glad we are."

They led him back to his stable.

"There is no bell like the bell of Atri," said the people. "It helps all who are in trouble. Even a horse may ring it."

Italian Tale.

101. The Summer-Maker

I

Once upon a time there was only one season in the whole year, and that season was winter.

Years and years went by, but it was always cold. Snow covered the ground, and ice covered the rivers. The trees were always bare. There were no leaves to dance and to play in the wind. There were no birds to sing, and no sweet flowers to bloom.

Ojeeg was a little Indian boy who lived in this land of snow. Big Hunter was his father.

Big Hunter did not mind the cold. He often went hunting and brought home a deer or a bear, to make a feast for his friends and for little Ojeeg.

Now, Ojeeg loved to hunt, too. He had a little bow and arrow, and often went out to hunt for food.

But he never could go far. He was a very little boy, and his small fingers always got numb with the cold.

Then he could not use the bow and arrow, so he had to go back to the wigwam.

He often cried because he had brought back no food. All the big Indian boys laughed because Ojeeg could not keep his little hands warm.

Ojeeg got very tired of this. One day he said to himself, "I am going to ask my father to make summer.

"Grandmother told me all about summer. She says father can use magic and can make summer if he will. Then I can stay out of doors all day. I can learn to be a big hunter."

That night Big Hunter came back to the wigwam with a fine bear.

Little Ojeeg went to meet his father. His eyes were full of tears.

"Father, help me," he said. "I am tired of the cold and the snow. It makes my fingers so numb that I cannot hold the bow and arrow.

"I want to hunt all day long, as you do. I want to bring home food for my mother."

His father smiled, for he was very fond of his little son.

"How can I help you?" he said. "You must learn to wait. You will grow, and your hands will get big and strong. Then they will not get so cold."

"I do not want to wait," said little Ojeeg. "I want you to make summer. Grandmother says you can. Do make summer, for me. Oh, do. Father, do! Then I can be a big hunter like you."

Big Hunter thought a long time. "It will be very hard to do what you ask," he said, "but I will try."

II

So Big Hunter made a great feast. He roasted a bear, and asked three of his friends to come to the feast.

Then he told them about little Ojeeg and his troubles.

"Will you go with me to make summer for him?" he asked.

"We will go," they said. "Then Ojeeg can hunt all day long. He will bring home a bear and make a feast for us."

Big Hunter and his three friends, Otter, Beaver, and Badger, started on their long journey. On and on they went, for many, many days, until they came to a high mountain. It almost touched the sky, it was so high.

Big Hunter and his friends climbed to the very top.

"We must make a hole in the sky," said Big Hunter. They stretched out their hands, but they could not reach the sky.

"We must jump," said Big Hunter. "Otter, you are a great jumper. You must try first."

So Otter jumped as high as he could, but he could not reach the sky. He fell back and rolled down the mountain.

"That is enough for me," he said. "I shall not try such a jump again." He ran home as fast as he could go.

Then it was Beaver's turn. He took a deep breath. Then he jumped—oh! how he jumped! But he could not reach the sky.

He had such a hard fall that he lay very still on the mountain-top.

"We must try another way," said Big Hunter to Badger. "You stand on the very top of the mountain, and I will climb upon your shoulders. Then I will jump."

So Badger stood like a rock. Then Big- Hunter climbed on the strong shoulders of his friend.

Then he jumped! No one had ever jumped so high before. He touched the sky!

He fell back, but Badger caught him in his strong arms. Big Hunter jumped again, and beat at the sky with his fists.

This time he made a little hole in the sky, and a warm breeze came through it.

Once more Big Hunter climbed on to the shoulders of his friend. Once more he gave a great jump.

This time he struck such a mighty blow that the sky opened.

Then down through the great hole rushed the birds and the soft, warm winds and summer, beautiful summer!

Away they went to the cold land of snow, where little Ojeeg waited.

The soft, warm air melted the snow and ice. Little brooks began to run over the stones. Rivers flowed and sparkled in the sun. Leaves came out on the trees. Flowers bloomed, and birds sang.

Then little Ojeeg hunted and fished as much as he wanted, and brought food home to his mother. He made a great feast for the Summer-Maker and his friends.

Little Ojeeg learned to be a great hunter, like his father, and the big boys laughed at him no more.

Ever since that time summer always comes once a year.

Indian Legend.

102. The Three Pigs

I

Once three little pigs said to their mother, "We are big enough to earn our own living. Let us get something to do."

"Very well," said Mother Pig. "But look out for the wolf!"

So they set out to earn their living.

The first pig met a man with some straw.

"Please give me some of that straw," said the little pig. "I want to build a house."

So the man gave him some straw, and the little pig built a straw house.

Along came the wolf. He knocked at the door, rap, rap, rap, and the little pig went to the window and looked out.

"Little pig, little pig, let me come in!" said the wolf.

"Not by the hair of my chinny chin chin. You are the wolf, and you can't come in!" said the little pig.

"Then I'll huff and I'll puff, and I'll blow your house in," said the wolf.

So he huffed and he puffed, and he blew the house in. Then he ate up the little pig.

The second little pig met a man with some sticks.

"Please give me some of those sticks," said the little pig. "I want to build a house."

So the man gave him some sticks, and the little pig built a house of sticks.

Along came the wolf. He knocked at the door, rap, rap, rap. The little pig went to the window and looked out. "Little pig, little pig, let me come in!" said the wolf.

"Not by the hair of my chinny chin chin. You are the wolf, and you can't come in!" said the little pig.

"Then I'll huff and I'll puff, and I'll blow your house in," said the wolf.

So he huffed and he puffed, and he puffed and he huffed, and he blew the house in. Then he ate up the little pig.

II

The third little pig met a man with some bricks.

"Please give me some bricks," said the little pig. "I want to build a house."

So the man gave him some bricks, and the little pig built a brick house.

Along came the wolf. He knocked at the door, rap, rap, rap. The little pig went to the window and looked out.

"Little pig, little pig, let me come in!" said the wolf.

"Not by the hair of my chinny chin chin. You are the wolf, and you can't come in!" said the little pig.

"Then I'll huff and I'll puff, and I'll blow your house in," said the wolf.

So he huffed and he puffed, and he huffed and he puffed, and he puffed and he huffed, but he could not blow the house in.

Then he said, "Little pig, do you want some turnips?"

"I like turnips very much," said the little pig. "Where are they?"

"Do you see that field?" said the wolf. "It has rows and rows of juicy turnips. I will come in the morning to show you the way, and we will get some of them for dinner."

"What time will you come?" asked the little pig.

"At six o'clock," answered the wolf.

But the little pig got up at five o'clock, and went to the field. He got a basket full of juicy turnips. Then he ran home.

At six o'clock along came the wolf.

"Little pig, are you ready?" he called.

"Oh, I went to the field at five o'clock," said the little pig. "I have a pot full of turnips on the fire. Don't you smell them?"

The wolf was angry, but he said, "Little pig, I know where there is an apple tree."

"Where?" asked the little pig.

"Do you see that garden?" said the wolf. "The apples are there, all red and ripe and ready to eat. I will come for you in the morning, and we will get some for dinner."

"What time will you come?" asked the little pig.

"At five o'clock," said the wolf.

But the little pig went to the garden at four o'clock and climbed the apple tree. He filled his basket with apples.

Just then, along came the wolf.

"Oho! I have you now!" he shouted.

The little pig was very much frightened, but he looked down and said, "These apples are so good that I will throw you one."

He threw an apple as far as he could. While the wolf was running to pick it up, the little pig jumped out of the tree and ran home with his basket of apples.

III

The next day the wolf came again. He said, "There is a fair in the town. Will you go there with me in the morning?"

"Oh, yes," said the little pig. "I will go to the fair. I need a churn. I will buy it at the fair. What time will you come for me?"

"At four o'clock," said the wolf.

But the little pig got up at three o'clock and went to the fair. He bought a fine churn.

"Now I will make nice yellow butter," he said to himself. "But I must hurry home before the wolf comes."

When he got to the top of the hill, he saw the wolf coming up. The little pig was very much frightened.

"What shall I do?" he said. "There is nothing to hide in except this churn."

So he got into the churn. Then the churn began to roll down the hill. Round and round and round it rolled.

When the wolf saw it coming he said, "What strange beast is this?"

He was so frightened that he turned and ran home, and the little pig was safe.

The next day the wolf came again.

"Did you go to the fair yesterday?" asked the little pig.

"No," said the wolf. "I was going to the fair, but I met a big round thing. I do not know what it was, but it looked like a strange beast.

"It rolled down the hill and frightened me so that I ran home."

"Oho! I frightened you, did I?" said the little pig. "That round thing was my churn. When I saw you I got into it and rolled down the hill."

The wolf was so angry that he said, "I will come down the chimney and eat you."

When the little pig heard this, he made a fire and put on a pot of water to heat. He took the lid off the pot when the wolf came down the chimney. The wolf fell into the pot, and after that he never again came to visit the little pig.

English Tale.

103. The House in the Woods

I

Once there was a poor wood-cutter who had a wife and three little girls.

He went into the woods every day to cut down trees. It was very hard work.

One day he said to his wife, "I shall be gone all day, for I must go a long way into the woods. I want our oldest girl to bring me a warm dinner."

"She might lose her way," said the mother.

"No, no!" said the father. "I will take a bag of grass seed with me. I will drop the seeds to show the way."

So the father went into the woods, and he dropped the seed to show the way.

At noon the oldest girl went to find him. She took some bread and a pail of hot soup.

She looked for the grass seed to show the way, but the blackbirds had eaten it all up. On and on she went. By and by, night came, and it was very dark in the woods.

"I am afraid!" she said. "I cannot find father, and I do not know the way home. I do not want to stay in the woods all night. What shall I do?"

All at once she saw a light shining through the trees. "That must be a house," she said.

"I will knock at the door and say that I am lost. Maybe I can stay all night."

So she walked on toward the light until she came to a tiny house.

Tap! Tap! Tap! she knocked at the door. "Come in!" said a gruff voice. She lifted the latch and went in.

An old woman was sitting in the room. There was a bright fire on the hearth. A rooster, a hen, and a speckled cow were lying before it.

"If you please," said the oldest girl, "I have lost my way. It is very dark in the woods. May I stay here all night?"

The old woman turned to the rooster, the hen, and the speckled cow.

"Shall we let her stay?" she asked.

The rooster crowed, the hen clucked, and the speckled cow said, "Moo!"

The old woman knew what they meant. She said, "You may stay, but you must work. Go into the kitchen and get us some supper."

The oldest girl did not want to work, but she went into the kitchen.

She made a dish of stew, and gave some to the old woman. She ate the rest, but she forgot to feed the rooster, the hen, and the cow.

Then she said, "I am sleepy. I want to go to bed."

"You must make the beds first," said the old woman. So she led her upstairs.

The oldest girl made her own bed, but she forgot to make the old woman's bed. Then she lay down and went to sleep.

By and by the old woman came upstairs. Her bed was not made, and she found the oldest girl asleep.

Then the old woman opened a large door in the floor. Bump! The oldest girl, the bed, and all, fell down into the cellar.

II

That night, when the wood-cutter got home, he was tired and hungry. "Where is our oldest girl?" he said. "I have had no dinner."

"I sent her with some hot dinner for you," said the mother, "but she did not come back. I am afraid she is lost."

"She will come home in the morning," said the wood-cutter. "She will find a place to sleep. The second girl must bring my dinner tomorrow."

"She might lose her way, too," said the mother.

"No, no!" said the wood-cutter. "I will take a bag of wheat, and drop some of it to show the way. It is larger than grass seed, and she can see it better."

So the next day the father went into the woods. He dropped the wheat as he went, but the birds ate it all up, so the second girl could not find the way.

She went on and on until it was dark. She heard the owls hoot and she was afraid.

Then she saw the same light shining through the trees that her older sister had seen, and she found the same tiny house. She went in and asked the old woman if she might stay all night.

The old woman turned to the rooster, the hen, and the speckled cow. "Shall we let her stay?" she asked.

The rooster crowed, the hen clucked, and the speckled cow said, "Moo!"

So the second girl stayed all night. She went into the kitchen and cooked some supper, but she forgot to feed the rooster, the hen, and the speckled cow.

Then she went upstairs and made her bed, but she was like her sister, and forgot to make the old woman's bed.

So the door in the floor opened, and bump! The second girl, the bed, and all, fell down into the cellar.

III

In the morning the wood-cutter said, "Our second girl must have lost her way, too. I have had no dinner for two days. Our youngest girl must bring my hot soup and bread today."

"She may lose her way, too," said the mother. "I have lost two girls! I cannot let her go!"

"No, no!" said the wood-cutter. "I will take a bag of peas with me this time. I will drop the peas to show the way. They are bigger than wheat, and she will be sure to see them. Then she will find the way."

So the wood-cutter went into the woods. He dropped the peas to show the way, but the birds ate them all up. The youngest girl could not find the way.

She went on and on until it was dark. Then she saw the light shining through the trees and she found the tiny house. She knocked on the door, as her sisters had done.

The old woman opened the door as she had done for the two older sisters.

The youngest girl spoke kindly to the rooster, the hen, and the speckled cow. She went close to them and patted them. Then she went into the kitchen and cooked the old woman's supper.

Now the youngest girl was kind-hearted, and she would not eat until the rooster, the hen, and the speckled cow had been fed. She brought corn for the rooster and the hen, and an armful of hay for the speckled cow.

Then she brought a pail full of cool water for them, and they drank as much as they wanted.

Then the youngest girl ate her supper. After supper she went upstairs to make the old woman's bed. She shook the bed well, and put clean sheets upon it. Then she made a bed for herself, and soon fell fast asleep.

IV

When she woke up, the sun was shining, and everything was changed.

She was in a beautiful room! The bed was made of ivory, and the chairs were all made of gold.

"Oh, oh!" she said. "This must be a dream. I shall wake by and by." She pinched herself to see if she was asleep, but she found that she was wide awake.

"I must get up and cook the old woman's breakfast," she said. "I must feed the rooster, the hen, and the speckled cow."

She ran downstairs and found herself in a wonderful room. In the center of the room was a great table. Someone was sitting at the table, but it was not the old woman. It was a beautiful Princess!

There was a bright fire on the hearth. The rooster, the hen, and the speckled cow were not lying by the fire, but three servants were bringing in dishes of food.

The youngest girl was so surprised that she did not know what to do.

"Come to me, dear little girl," said the Princess, "and I will tell you all about it. My father is a king. A witch changed me into an old woman, and my castle into a tiny house. She changed my three servants into a rooster, a hen, and a speckled cow.

"No one could change us back but a kind girl. You were kind. You cooked my supper and made my bed. You did not forget the rooster, the hen, and the speckled cow.

"So last night we were all changed back again. We were changed because you were kind to us. I am a Princess again, and the rooster, the hen, and the speckled cow are servants.

"We are all happy again. You must live with us, and we will make you happy, too."

"But I must go home now," said the youngest girl. "My father and mother will be sad. I must help them find my sisters who were lost in the woods."

"Do not run away," said the Princess. "I will go with you, and I will help your father and mother. Then I will take you to live with me. But first let us find your sisters. Come with me."

So she opened the cellar door. Out came the oldest girl and the second girl. How happy they were to see their sister! Then they all went together to the wood-cutter's house.

Old Tale.

104. The Lad Who Went to the North Wind

I

Once there was a woman who was very poor. One day she sent her only son to the pantry to get some meal.

As the lad got the meal, along came the North Wind, puffing and blowing. He caught up the meal, and away it went through the air.

Then the lad went back to the pantry for some more meal. Along came the North Wind again. He caught up the meal with a puff, and away it went again.

The lad went back the third time for some meal, and the third time the North Wind puffed it away.

Then the lad became angry. "I will go to the North Wind and make him give me back my meal!" he said.

He walked and walked, until at last he came to the North Wind's house.

"Good-day, North Wind!" said the lad.

"Good-day!" said the North Wind, in a gruff voice. "What do you want?"

"I want you to give me back the meal you took from me," said the lad. "We are poor, and we need it."

"Your meal is not here," said the North Wind. "But since you are poor, I will give you this cloth. When you want food, you must say, 'Cloth, spread yourself. Serve up some good things to eat.' Then you will have all the food you want."

"Thank you, North Wind," said the lad. "That is better than the meal."

So he set out for home.

The way was so long that he could not get home in one day. When evening came, he went to an inn to stay all night.

"How hungry my long walk has made me!" he said to himself. "I will put my cloth on the table, as the North Wind told me to do."

Then he said, "Cloth, spread yourself. Serve up good things to eat."

The cloth did as it was told, and the lad had a fine supper. All the people in the inn said, "What a wonderful cloth!" The inn- keeper said to himself, "I should like to have this cloth."

So when the lad was asleep he took it away, and put another cloth in its place. It looked just like the cloth from the North Wind, but it could not serve up even a dry crust.

In the morning the lad took the cloth, and went off with it. That day he got home to his mother.

"Where have you been, and what is that cloth which you are bringing home with you?" asked his mother.

"Oh, I have been to the North Wind's house. I went to get the meal back," said the lad, "but he told me that he did not have our meal.

"He gave me this cloth, instead. Whenever I say, 'Cloth, spread yourself. Serve up good things to eat,' I get all the food I want."

"That may be true," said his mother. "But I shall not believe it until I see it with my own eyes."

So the lad laid the cloth on the table and said, "Cloth, spread yourself. Serve up good things to eat." But the cloth did not serve up even a dry crust. The lad was so surprised that he could not say a word. How his mother laughed at him!

"I must go to the North Wind again," said the lad. Away he went.

"What do you want now?" said the North Wind, when the lad knocked at his door.

"I want my meal," said the lad. "This cloth is not worth a penny."

"I have no meal," said the North Wind, "but I will give you this ram. It makes money. Just say, 'Ram, ram! Make money!' Then you shall have all the gold you want."

"That is better than meal," said the lad.

So off he went, and he stayed at the inn that night, too. After supper he wanted to see if the North Wind was right.

As soon as he said, "Ram, ram! Make money!" he had all the gold he wanted.

When the inn-keeper saw the ram making money, he said to himself, "I want that ram."

He had a ram that looked just like this one, so he took the lad's ram and put his own ram in its place.

In the morning the lad went away. When he got home he said to his mother, "After all, the North Wind is a good fellow. Now he has given me a ram

that can make gold. I say, "Ram, ram! Make money!"
Then I have all the gold I want."

"That may be true," said his mother. "But I shall
believe it when I see the gold."

"Ram, ram! Make money!" said the lad. But the
ram did not make even a penny.

The lad's mother laughed at him this time, too.

So the lad went to the North Wind again.

"I want my meal." he said. "The ram you gave me
is not worth a penny."

"I have no meal," said the North Wind. "I have
nothing to give you except this old stick. When you
say, 'Stick, stick! Lay on!' it will lay on. When you want
it to stop, you must say, 'Stick, stick! Stop!'"

So the lad took the stick, and went to the inn
again. He said to himself, "I think I know who has my
cloth and my ram. I will see if I can get them back."

So he lay down on a bench. "I will keep so still
that I shall seem to be asleep," he said. "But I will
keep a very close watch."

By and by the inn-keeper saw the stick. He said, "I
have a wonderful cloth and a wonderful ram. Perhaps
this is a wonderful stick. I think I will take it."

So he went away and found a stick that looked like
the stick from the North Wind. Then he came back to
change the two sticks.

Then the lad said, "Stick, stick! Lay on!"

The stick began to beat the inn-keeper. He jumped over tables and benches, but he could not get away from the stick.

"Lad, lad, stop the stick!" he cried. "You shall have your cloth and your ram."

So the lad said, "Stick, stick! Stop!"

Then he took the cloth and the ram and the stick, and went home.

He said, "The North Wind has paid me well for my meal. This time my mother cannot laugh at me."

Norse Tale.

105. The Months

January brings the snow,
See the snow men in a row.

February days are longer,
Nights are cold, and winds are stronger.

March brings breezes loud that shake
The little flowers to make them wake.

April brings both sun and rain
To make the whole world green again.

May brings songs of bird and bee,
Joy for you and joy for me.

June brings buttercups and roses,
See her hands all filled with posies.

Hot July brings cooling showers
For thirsty fields and trees and flowers.

August days are full of heat,
Then fruits grow ripe for us to eat.

September brings the golden-rod
And milkweed flying from its pod.

In October, nuts are brown,
And yellow leaves fall slowly down.

November brings the chilly rain.
Whirling winds, and frost again.

Cold December ends the year
With Christmas tree, and Christmas cheer.

Adapted from Mother Goose.

Who Has Seen The Wind?

Who has seen the wind?
    Neither I nor you;
But when the leaves hang trembling,
    The wind is passing through.

Who has seen the wind?
    Neither you nor I;
But when the trees bow down their heads,
    The wind is passing by.

Christina G. Rossetti.

106. Come, Little Leaves

"Come, little leaves," said the wind one day,
"Come o'er the meadows with me and play;
Put on your dresses of red and gold;
Summer is gone, and the days grow cold."

Soon as the leaves heard the wind's loud call,
Down they came fluttering, one and all;
Over the brown fields they danced and flew,
Singing the glad little songs they knew.

Dancing and whirling, the little leaves went;
Winter had called them, and they were content.
Soon fast asleep in their earthy beds
The snow laid a white blanket over their heads.

George Cooper.

The Leaf That Was Afraid

One day the wind was talking to a little leaf. He made her sigh and cry as leaves sometimes do when the wind is about.

"What is the trouble, little leaf? Why do you cry?" asked the twig on which the leaf grew.

"The wind told me," said the leaf, "that some day he would blow me away from you." Then she sighed again.

The twig told the branch, and the branch told the tree. The tree laughed and said, "Do not be afraid, little leaf. You need not go until you want to."

Then the leaf stopped crying, and was happy. All summer she grew and grew.

One day in the fall, she looked at the other leaves and saw how beautiful they were. Some were yellow and some were red and some were both colors.

Then the leaf asked the tree, "Why are the other leaves red and yellow?"

"Their work is done," said the tree, "and they are so happy that they dress in beautiful colors. They are ready to fly away."

Then the leaf wanted to go with the other leaves. While she was thinking about it, she, too, grew very beautiful.

One day the wind came to her again. "Are you ready to go now?" he asked.

"Yes," answered the leaf. "I am ready to fly away with the other leaves."

The wind blew very hard. Away went the leaf with many other leaves, to cover up some little seeds, and to keep them warm all winter.

Then the little leaf fell asleep.

Henry Ward Beecher, Adapted.

107. The Snow Man

See, here's a man so fond of cold
He cannot stand the heat, I'm told;
The breezes of a summer day
Would simply make him melt away.

He loves the coldest winds that blow,
This pale-faced man who's made of snow.
He's frozen stiff as he can be;
That's why he stays with us, you see.

His friends are very, very few;
He's far too cold for me or you;

And he would be completely lost
Without his faithful friend, Jack Frost.

Together they must always be;
They cannot live apart, you see.
And when Old Jack Frost goes away,
The Snow Man can no longer stay.

Rebecca B. Foresman.

108. The Dolls' Thanksgiving Dinner

I

"Why can't dolls have a Thanksgiving dinner as well as little girls?" asked Polly Pine.

"I don't know why," said Mother, laughing. "Go and dress them in their best clothes. Get the doll house swept and dusted, and the table ready. Then I'll see about a dinner."

"Oh, how nice!" said Polly Pine.

The doll house stood in Polly's play-room. It was very big and very beautiful.

Polly Pine swept the rooms with her tiny broom. Then she dusted them. She set the table for dinner with the very best dishes and silver. She put a tiny vase, with a little flower in it, in the center of the table, and she placed wee napkins at each plate.

When the doll house was clean and the table was set she dressed Susan in a pink dress, Dora Jane in gray, and Hannah in yellow.

Then she placed them around the table, each one in her own chair.

"Be very careful, Susan!" she said. "Remember not to eat with your knife. Dora Jane, do not leave your teaspoon in your cup when you drink your tea."

Just then Mother came in with the dolls' Thanksgiving dinner.

There was a small piece of turkey to put on the plate, before Hannah. Hannah was the oldest, and always carved the meat for the other dolls.

There were little dishes of potato and cranberry sauce. There was cake on a tiny plate. Then there was the smallest squash pie ever seen.

Polly Pine hopped up and down with joy. She set everything on the table. Then she ran away to get ready for her own dinner.

She put on a pretty white dress and went downstairs.

II

Some friends had been asked to come to dinner, and they were all there. Polly was very fond of them, and she had a fine time at the dinner table.

One of the gentlemen could change his big napkin into a white rabbit. Polly thought this was so funny that she forgot all about the dolls' Thanksgiving dinner.

At last it was time for the dessert, and the nuts and the raisins were brought in and put on the table.

Then Polly remembered. She jumped down from her chair. "Oh, Mother!" she said. "May I go to see if the dolls liked their dinner?'"

Mother told the visitors about the Thanksgiving dinner in the doll house. Everybody wanted to go with Polly, so they all went upstairs.

There sat the dolls, just as their little mother had left them—but they had eaten nearly all the dinner!

Pieces of food were scattered all over the table. The bread and the cake were all gone, and the crust of the little squash pie was eaten all around.

"Well, this is strange!" said Father.

Just then they heard a scratching sound in the doll house, and a little gray mouse jumped out from under the table.

He ran out of the front door and down the steps. In a moment he was gone, nobody knew where.

There was another tiny mouse in the doll house under a chair. A third one was under the bed, with a poor, frightened gray tail sticking out.

All of the mice ran safely away. They looked as though they had eaten a big dinner.

"Shall I get the cat?" asked Mother.

"No," said Father. "Why can't a poor little mouse have a Thanksgiving dinner as well as we?"

Isabel Gordon Curtis, Adapted.

109. The Golden Cobwebs

I

It was just before Christmas. A beautiful Christmas Tree stood in a pretty room of a pleasant home.

The Tree was trimmed with popcorn, silver nuts, candies, and little candles. Its branches were full of toys.

The doors of the room were locked so that the children could not get in.

"We must not let them see the Tree until Christmas morning," said the house-mother.

But there were many other little people in the house. They had seen the Tree already. The big black kitty had seen it with her great green eyes. The little gray kitty had seen it with her round blue eyes. The big house dog had seen it with his kind brown eyes. The yellow canary had seen it with his wise bright eyes.

Even the wee, wee mice had peeped just once when no one was by.

But there was someone who had not seen the Christmas Tree. It was the little gray spider.

You see, the spiders lived in the corners. Some had homes in the warm corners of the attic. Some made their webs in the dark corners of the nice cellar. They wanted to see the Christmas Tree, too.

But just before Christmas the house-mother cleaned the house. She swept and dusted everywhere. Her broom went into all the corners of all the rooms—poke, poke, poke!

Of course the spiders had to run. Dear dear, how the spiders had to run! Not a single spider could stay in the house while it was so clean.

Some ran up the attic stairs and hid in the sunny attic; some ran down the cellar stairs and hid in the dark cellar. They could not see the Christmas Tree.

The spiders like to see all there is to see. So of course they were very, very sad. At last they went to the Christmas Fairy and told her all about it.

"All the other little house-people have seen the Christmas Tree," they said. "But we cannot see it. We love beautiful things, too. Dear Christmas Fairy, help us to see the Christmas Tree!"

The Christmas Fairy said, "You shall see the Tree. Just wait."

II

The day before Christmas everyone was busy. No one was in the room with the Christmas Tree. So the Christmas Fairy said to the spiders, "Now you may go in. You may look as long as you like."

So the spiders came creepy, creepy, down the attic stairs. They came creepy, creepy, up the cellar stairs. They came creepy, creepy, along the halls. They went creepy, creepy, into the pretty room.

The fat mother spiders and the old father spiders were there. All the little teeny, tiny curly, baby spiders were there.

And then they looked! Round and round the Tree they went, creepy, crawly. They looked and looked and looked. Oh, what a good time they had!

"What a beautiful Tree!" said the old father spiders. "What a beautiful, beautiful Tree!" said the fat mother spiders.

"What a beautiful, beautiful, beautiful Tree!" said the teeny, tiny, curly, baby spiders.

They looked at everything they could see from the floor. Then they ran up the Tree to see some more. They ran all over the Tree, creepy, crawly, creepy, crawly.

They looked at every single thing. They ran up and down and in and out. They ran over every branch and twig.

They ran over every one of the pretty toys on the Tree.

They went round and round the doll.

They went over and over the drum. They went in and out of the trumpet. They went up and down the jumping-jack.

They stayed until they had seen everything. Then they went away happy. They had seen the beautiful Christmas Tree, too.

In the still, dark night the Christmas Fairy came.

"I must see if the beautiful Tree is all ready for Christmas morning," she said. "The children will be up very early to see it."

But when she looked at it, what do you think? It was all covered with cobwebs!

Every place the little spiders had been, they had left a spider-web. And you know they had been just everywhere!

The Tree was covered from top to bottom with spider-webs. They hung from the branches. They went round and round the toys. The Christmas Fairy could hardly see the doll's face.

What could the Fairy do? "Now I see why the house-mother drove all the spiders away," she said. "It will never do to have cobwebs on the Christmas Tree. No, indeed! What shall I do?"

So the Christmas Fairy thought and thought. "Oh, now I have a plan!" she said. She touched the spider-webs with her fairy wand and turned them all to gold. Was not that a beautiful trimming? They shone and shone all over the Christmas Tree.

And ever since that time the Christmas Tree is always trimmed with golden cobwebs.

Robert Haven Schauffler, Adapted.

110. The Easter Rabbit

I

Once upon a time, many years ago, the winter had been long and cold.

"What makes Spring so late?" said all the little children. "Let us go to the woods and see if she has come yet."

But when they got there they found the woods bare and cold. There were no birds or flowers, anywhere, and only Jack Frost and North Wind were playing among the trees.

Poor children! They went back to their homes with sad hearts and faces.

At last Spring came. When Jack Frost and North Wind saw her, they waved good-bye and ran away.

Soon the birds were building their nests, the flowers were peeping up out of the ground, and the tree buds were bursting.

But the children, where were they?

"Why don't the children come to the woods?" said Spring. "Last year and every other year they came to play with the birds and the flowers and the animals."

"It is lonely without them," said the birds. "They will not hear our beautiful songs."

"If they do not come soon," said the flowers, "our blossoms will all be gone."

All the baby rabbits and squirrels and foxes said, "We want to see the children. We want to hide in our holes and peep out at them as they pass."

"Perhaps they do not know we are here," said Spring. "Robin, will you tell them?"

"I am too busy building a nest for my little ones," said the robin. "Send the fox. His little ones are already here."

"Will you go, Red Fox?" said Spring.

"I dare not go," said the fox. "The people will think I have come to steal the chickens."

"That is true," said Spring. "We cannot send you. Black Bear, will you go?"

"I am so big and I look so fierce," said the bear, "that I would frighten the children. Besides, I am so thin and hungry after sleeping all winter that I must eat and eat and eat all day long. Ask the rabbit to go. Children all love rabbits."

Now, the rabbit is very timid, but he felt so proud to hear that all the children loved him, that he said he would go. Then he thought of the dogs. "Oh! But the dogs!" he said. "The dogs will catch me."

"You can go at night, when all the dogs are asleep," said Spring.

"So I can," said the rabbit. "I will go tonight."

II

So they made a big basket of twigs and leaves, and lined it with soft green grass. Then each bird brought an egg from her nest, until the basket was nearly full.

There were blue eggs, and speckled eggs, and brown eggs. How pretty they looked! Then they covered the eggs over with early spring flowers, and tied the basket on bunny's back.

When evening came, the rabbit set off for the town, hippity-hop, hippity-hop. How strange and quiet it was in the town when everyone was asleep.

Bunny went to the first house where a child lived. He made a little nest of the soft green grass, and put into it one pretty egg and one spring flower.

He put the nest on the door step, and hopped on to the next house, and the next, and the next. When the sun came up, he hopped back to the woods, a happy bunny.

"Why, Spring is here! Spring is here!" said the children when they saw the pretty nests on their door steps next morning. "We were afraid that she was not coming this year. But, see, here are the tracks of a rabbit's feet. He must have brought us the message."

So off they ran to the woods, crying with happy voices, "Hurrah for bunny! Hurrah for bunny! For Spring is here at last, and bunny has come to tell us!"

Old Tale.

111. America

My country, 'tis of thee,
Sweet land of Liberty,
   Of thee I sing;
Land where my fathers died,
Land of the pilgrim's pride,
From every mountain side
   Let Freedom ring.

My native country, thee—
Land of the noble free—
   Thy name I love;
I love thy rocks and rills,
Thy woods and templed hills;
My heart with rapture thrills,
   Like that above.

Let music swell the breeze,
And ring from all the trees
   Sweet Freedom's song;
Let mortal tongues awake,
Let all that breathe partake,
Let rocks their silence break—
   The sound prolong.

Samuel F. Smith.

The Flag

Hats off!

Along the street there comes

A blare of bugles, a ruffle of drums,

A flash of color beneath the sky.

Hats off!

The flag is passing by!

Hats off!

Along the street there comes

A blare of bugles, a ruffle of drums,

And loyal hearts are beating high.

Hats off!

The flag is passing by!

Henry R. Bennett.

112. Joan and Pierre

Joan and Pierre were two little French children. They lived in a small village that had been torn to pieces by the guns of the Great War.

They had not seen each other for a long time. One day they met on the street.

"Oh, Joan!" said Pierre, "What a beautiful new coat you have. Where did you get it? Did St. Nicholas bring it to you?"

"Oh, no, Pierre." said Joan. "St. Nicholas did not bring it to me. He didn't know where to find me this year, because we are living in a cellar now.

"I am glad you like my coat. I have a new cap, too. It is so nice and warm. And my little sister has some new shoes. We are very happy now. We get good food every day, so that we are never hungry anymore."

"Oh, where do you get the food, Joan? Do tell me," said Pierre. "I am hungry now, and I am very cold, too."

"Come with me, poor little Pierre," said Joan. "I will get you food and clothes."

She took him to the other end of the little torn-up village. There stood a long, low house. They could see it from very far away, as there were no other houses standing on the street. They could see the fluttering of a red, white, and blue flag while they were yet far away.

"Oh, I see the house." said Pierre. "It has our flag on top. We must salute it."

"Oh, no," said Joan. "That is not our flag. But we must both salute it. That is the American Flag. It is red, white, and blue like ours. My father says it made him very happy the first time he saw it in the trenches."

"My father didn't come back from the war," said little Pierre.

Soon they reached the long, low house. Then they saw another flag flying. It had a red cross on a field of white.

Joan took Pierre into the house, where he saw piles of hats and coats and shoes. There were some toys, too. Pierre was given nice, warm clothes, a pair of shoes, and a cap. He got some warm food, too.

"I like this house," said Pierre. "I think I'll come here every day. I'll bring my little brother, too. What is the name of this house, Joan?"

"This is the house of the Junior Red Cross," said Joan. "The little boys and girls of America send us these things."

"Hurrah for the Junior Red Cross," said Pierre.

Edna V. Riddleberger.

113. Lincoln and His Dog

Once there was a kind-hearted lad named Abraham Lincoln. His friends called him Abe, for short.

He lived with his father, mother, and sister in a cabin on a little farm. The cabin had only one room. They were very poor, and his father had a hard time to make a living.

One day he said to his family, "I have sold the farm. This land is too poor. We will move to some place where the soil is better for farming. There we can make a better living."

As there were no railroads in those days, people had to move from place to place in wagons. So the Lincoln family put their rough furniture into a covered wagon. With two strong oxen to pull it, they started on their journey.

It was near the end of winter, and the roads were deep with mud. Often the heavy wagon sank down almost to the hubs of the wheels. Through the woods they went, and up and down the hills. The journey was slow and tiresome.

In those days there were no bridges over the streams they had to cross. So the strong oxen had to pull the wagon across the frozen streams. They broke through the ice with every step.

It was a long, cold, hard journey. How glad they would all be to reach the little home at the end. But they knew it would be only a rough cabin like the one they had left.

Abe walked along by the wagon. Sometimes he patted the faithful oxen as they pulled their heavy load.

By his side trotted his little dog. The dog really seemed to like the hard journey. For there were many squirrels to send hurrying up the trees. There were rabbits to chase, too. It was just fun for the dog.

But one day the little dog chased a rabbit far off into the woods. While he was gone, the oxen pulled the wagon, with the family inside, through a frozen stream. The thin ice cracked under their heavy feet and then floated off down the stream.

The Lincoln family had gone on some distance when they heard a loud barking behind them. Looking back, they saw the timid little dog on the other side of the stream, barking with all his might. He was running up and down the bank.

The lad, Abe, ran back and tried to coax him to cross on the thin ice. But the frightened little animal could not be coaxed. He was afraid the ice would not bear even his light weight.

"We shall have to go on without him," said the older ones of the family. "The roads are so deep with mud that the oxen cannot turn back."

"But he will starve, or freeze," said little Abe. "We can't be so cruel as that. Listen how he whines!"

Abe sat down and quickly pulled off his heavy shoes and stockings. Then he waded back through the cold water. The happy little dog jumped all over him in his joy.

He took the shivering little animal in his arms, and waded again through the stream. Soon he overtook the slow oxen.

All the rest of the journey the little dog kept close by the boy's side. He had found out that a good friend is worth more than many squirrels.

This kind-hearted lad, Abraham Lincoln, became one of our greatest presidents. The really great are always kind.

114. The Little Cook

Betty lived in the South, long, long ago. She was only ten years old, but she liked to help her mother.

She had learned to do many things. She could knit and sew and spin; but best of all she liked to cook.

One day Betty was alone at home, because her father and mother and brother had gone to town to see a wonderful sight.

The great George Washington was visiting the South. He was going from town to town, riding in a great white coach drawn by four milk-white horses. A coachman sat on a high seat in front and drove them.

Four horsemen rode ahead of the coach to clear the way, and four others rode behind it. They were all dressed in white and gold.

Great crowds of people waited at every town for Washington. When they saw him coming they clapped their hands and sang songs of welcome.

Little girls threw flowers before him as he rode along. Little boys dressed like soldiers, with fife and drum, marched to meet him. Betty's brother Robert was one of these boys.

But Betty could not see this wonderful sight. Someone had to stay at home to keep the house.

"I will stay, Mother," Betty had said. "Robert must march with the boys. I can keep the house, and I will cook supper for you. I will have it all ready when you get home."

After they were all gone Betty was very sad. Oh, how she wanted to go to town!

But little Betty must stay at home all day. She could never see the great George Washington, the first President of the United States.

She sat on a bench on the shady porch, and felt very sad and lonely. All her work was done, and it was only nine o'clock. How could she bear the long, long day!

"Oh, if I could only see George Washington!" she said to herself.

But what sound was that? Someone was coming!

Four horsemen were galloping along the road that led to town. A great white coach drawn by four horses came after them. Then came more horsemen.

Betty's heart stood still, for they all stopped at the gate.

A tall man stepped from the coach and came up the walk. Betty got up to meet him, and made a curtsy as he reached the steps.

"Good morning, my little maid," said the tall man. "I know it is late, but can you give me some breakfast?"

Betty's cheeks grew rosy, and she made another curtsy.

"I will try, sir," she said. "Father and mother and brother Robert have gone to town to see the great George Washington. I am the only one at home."

"You do not need any help," said the tall man. "I am sure you are as quick as you are pretty. Just get a breakfast for me. Then I promise you that you shall see Washington before your brother does."

Betty's heart beat fast.

"I will do the best I can, sir," she said.

She went to work with quick hands and feet. She put wood on the fire and hung a kettle of water over it. Then she spread the table with a white cloth and put on the very best dishes and silver. She brought fresh honey and bread.

Then Betty ran to the cool spring-house for golden butter and rich milk. She cut thin slices of ham and put new-laid eggs into the boiling water.

The hungry stranger had such a fine breakfast that when he left the table he leaned over and kissed Betty.

"Now, my dear little cook," he said, "you may tell your brother Robert that you saw Washington before he did, and that he kissed you, too."

Lutie Andrews McCorkle, Adapted.

115. How Buttercups Came

Once there was an old man who lived all by himself. He had a great bag full of shining gold. He did not want to give away any of it, so he lived far back in the woods.

One night a robber came while the old man was asleep, and stole all the gold.

There was a hole in the bag in which the money had been kept, and as the robber rode away, the money fell out through the hole.

Early in the morning a little fairy came walking through the woods.

When she saw the pieces of money on the ground, she said, "If I leave them here, the old man will come and pick them up again. So I will change them into golden flowers."

Then she touched each piece of gold, and up sprang bright golden flowers. She called the flowers "Buttercups."

This is the way the beautiful golden buttercups came into the world.

Old Tale.

Daisies

At evening when I go to bed
I see the stars shine overhead;
They are the little daisies white
That dot the meadow of the night.

And often while I'm dreaming so,
Across the sky the Moon will go;
It is a lady, sweet and fair,
Who comes to gather daisies there.

For, when at morning I arise,
There's not a star left in the skies;
She's picked them all and dropped them down
Into the meadows of the town.

Frank Dempster Sherman.

116. The Kind Old Oak

It was almost time for winter to come.

The little birds had gone far away, for they were afraid of the cold. They had gone where it was warm and where there was plenty to eat.

There was no green grass in the fields and all the pretty flowers in the garden had gone to sleep for the winter.

Many of the trees had dropped their leaves. Cold winter with its ice and snow would soon be in the woods.

Some beautiful little violets were still in bloom near the foot of an old oak tree. They loved the old tree, for it had often sheltered them from the storms.

"Dear old oak," said the violets one day, "what shall we do to save ourselves? Winter is coming, and we are afraid that we shall die of cold."

"Do not be afraid," said the oak. "Close your yellow eyes and go to sleep. I will take care of you, so winter cannot harm you."

So the violets closed their eyes and went to sleep. Then the great tree dropped its leaves one by one until they had a nice warm covering.

Soon Jack Frost arrived with ice and snow, but he could not harm the little violets, because the kind old oak tree had taken care of them with a warm coat of leaves. They were safe.

There they slept and dreamed happy dreams until spring came. Then the warm rains and the sunshine came and woke them.

Old Tale.

Clovers

The clovers have no time to play;
They feed the cows and make the hay,
They trim the lawn and help the bees
Until the sun shines through the trees.

And then they lay aside their cares,
And fold their hands to say their prayers.

And bow their tired little heads,
And go to sleep in clover beds.

Then, when the day dawns clear and blue.
They wake and wash their hands in dew;
And as the sun climbs up the sky,
They hold them up and let them dry;
And then to work the livelong day,
For clovers have no time to play.

Helena Leeming Jeliffe.

117. The Girl Who Was Changed to a Sunflower

Clytie was a beautiful water-maiden who lived far down in the deep sea-caves. Her hair shone like gold in the green sea.

"Your hair is as bright as Apollo's golden chariot," her mother said one day. Clytie was playing with the shells on the floor of the sea-cave, and her yellow hair floated around her pretty head.

"Who is Apollo?" asked Clytie.

"He is the sun-god," said her mother. "He lives above the sea. Every day he drives the chariot of the sun straight across the sky."

"Why does he do that?" asked Clytie.

"He brings the bright sun and the day into the world," said her mother.

"When he begins his journey, it is morning in the sun-land. When he is high up in the heavens, it is noon.

"When he drives down the western sky, it is evening, and when he leads the sun- horses away to rest, it is night."

"Some day," said Clytie, "I shall go up to the sun-land to see Apollo, the sun-god."

So one day, when Clytie had grown to be a tall maiden, she left the sea-caves. She went up to the bright sun-land, and walked in a beautiful meadow by the sea.

Apollo, the great sun-god, was just getting into his golden chariot. He was very tall and beautiful.

The wild horses of the sun pranced and neighed and pulled at the reins. But Apollo held them with his strong hands and drove the chariot across the sky.

Clytie watched the sun-god all that day. When night came she did not go back to her cool sea-home.

The next day she watched again.

"I want to live in this beautiful sun-land," she said. "It is dark in the deep sea-caves. How can I bear to go back to them? Oh, how I wish I could always watch Apollo in his golden chariot!"

For nine days Clytie stood in the meadow. She tasted neither food nor drink. Her golden hair hung over her shoulders, and her face was always turned to the shining chariot of the sun.

She watched it as it started in the east. She lifted her head to see it as it climbed high in the heavens. She turned to look at it as it drove down the west.

Then a strange thing happened. Clytie changed. She was no longer a beautiful maiden, but she was a tall and slender plant.

Her pretty face became a flower. Her bright golden hair turned to yellow petals that looked like the rays of the sun.

Every morning the flower turned to see the sun rise. It lifted up its golden head to see the sun at noon, and turned to watch the sun set in the west.

For Clytie was changed to a sunflower.

Greek Legend.

118. The Fairy Shoemaker

I

Once there was a boy named Tom, who wanted to catch the Fairy Shoemaker.

"Do not try it," said his mother. "He is a tricky elf."

"Oh, but I must try!" said Tom. "The Fairy Shoemaker can tell me where there is a pot of gold. He can make me rich. I want to get the pot of gold."

"But how can you catch him?" asked his mother. "Can you keep your eyes on him all the time? You know, if you look away just once—pop! He is gone."

"I know I can catch him," said Tom. "I will go every day to look in the meadow, and in the woods. I will look and listen. Some day I shall hear his hammer.

"Then I will tiptoe softly until I see him. I will keep my eyes on him. I will not look away once. I will make him tell me where the pot of gold is. Then we shall be rich."

"Well, good luck to you," said his mother. "But I think you will get a pot of gold sooner if you earn it."

So every day Tom looked for the Fairy Shoemaker—on the hill, in the meadow, and in the woods. He listened for the sound of his tiny hammer and his song.

One day, when he had walked a long time, he was very tired and lay down on the hill to rest. All at once he heard something:

"Tip-tap, rip-rap,
Tick-a-tack-too."

It was the hammer of the Fairy Shoemaker. Tom put his ear close to the hill. He could hear a shrill voice singing:

"This way, that way,
So we make a shoe;
Getting rich every stitch,
Tick-a-tack-too."

It was the Fairy Shoemaker's Song. Tom's heart beat fast. Now, if he could only catch the elf, he could get the pot of gold. But first he must see him. Then he must keep his eyes on him. If he looked away once—pop! The tricky elf would be gone.

He went on tiptoe around the hill so quietly that he did not make a sound. There, in a little grassy spot, was a tiny old man. He was only a foot tall, and his face was full of wrinkles.

He wore a little leather apron, and in his lap was the little shoe he was making.

"Tip-tap, rip-rap,

Tick-a-tack-too,"

went his tiny hammer. Yes! It was the Fairy Shoemaker!

Tom's heart was full of joy. Oh, yes! He would keep his eyes on the elf. He would not look away once. Then he would get the pot of gold.

"Good morning!" said Tom. The Fairy Shoemaker did not say a word. Tom went closer to him.

"That is a fine shoe you are making," he said. The Fairy Shoemaker did not say a word.

Tom went closer still. "Show me the pot of gold!" he said. "Where is it?"

"Wait a minute," said the Fairy Shoemaker. "Let me take a pinch of snuff first."

He got out his snuff-box and took a big pinch. He snuffed it up his nose.

Then he held out the box to Tom. "Take a pinch yourself," he said. But Tom was wise. He knew that the elf was tricky.

"He thinks I will look away," he said to himself. "But I will not look at the box, oh, no! I will not take my eyes off his face."

So he put his hands out to feel for the box. Puff! The Fairy Shoemaker threw the snuff into Tom's eyes and nose and mouth.

"Ker-choo!" sneezed Tom. "Ker-choo! Ker-choo! Ker-choo!" The tears rolled down his cheeks.

"KER-CHOO!" He gave a big sneeze, and his eyes shut up tight. Pop! The Fairy Shoemaker was gone!

"Just so!" said his mother, when Tom got home. "What did I tell you? See how red your eyes are! And how you sneeze! The Fairy Shoemaker is a tricky elf. You had better try to earn your pot of gold, instead of hunting for the Fairy Shoemaker."

II

But Tom was not ready to give up. He wanted to get the pot of gold. He wanted to be rich.

"I have seen the Fairy Shoemaker once," he said. "I may see him again."

So every day Tom looked for him—on the hill, in the meadow, and in the woods. And one day, he heard him again by the ditch in the meadow.

"Tip-tap, rip-rap,

Tick-a-tack-too."

It was the Fairy Shoemaker's hammer.

He listened again. He could hear a shrill voice singing:

"Scarlet leather sewed together,

This will make a shoe;

Getting rich every stitch,

Tick-a-tack-too."

Tom walked quietly up to the ditch. The elf was sitting on a little stool. He was putting a heel on a little shoe.

"Tip-tap, rip-rap,

Tick-a-tack-too,"

went his tiny hammer. He was so busy that Tom got very close to him.

"That is a fine shoe," he said. The Fairy Shoemaker looked up. "Thank you kindly," he said.

"Whose shoe is it?" asked Tom.

"That is my business," said the Fairy Shoemaker.

Tom went nearer and nearer. He kept his eyes on the elf's face. "Why do you work so hard?" he said.

"That is my business, too," said the elf "You ought to work a little harder yourself. See what those cows are doing! They are breaking into the corn."

Tom had seen no cows. He was so surprised that he almost turned to look. Then he said, "Oho! That is just a trick to make me look away." He kept his eyes on the elf's face. He went nearer still, and then— jump! He caught the elf in his hand.

"Now I have you," said Tom. "Where is the pot of gold? I shall never let you go until you tell me."

"Come on, then," said the elf. "We must go to the woods. Then I will show you where the pot of gold is."

So they went across fields and ditches and bogs.

Tom held the elf in his hand all the way and kept his eyes on him. He could not see his steps. He slipped and stumbled and fell. It was not a pleasant walk, as you can see.

When at last they came to the woods, Tom said, "Where is the pot of gold?"

"There it is," said the Fairy Shoemaker, pointing to a tree. "Dig under the roots and you will find a great pot of gold."

"Dig under the roots!" cried Tom. "But I have no spade."

"Go home and get one," said the elf.

"I will do that," said Tom. "But first I will tie my yellow neck scarf around the tree. Then I can find it when I come back."

So he tied his scarf around the tree.

"Now put me down. I must go home," said the Fairy Shoemaker.

"I will put you down." said Tom, "if you will promise not to touch the scarf I tied on the tree."

"I promise," said the Fairy Shoemaker. "I will not touch it, and no one shall touch it. May I go?"

Tom put him down. "Yes, you may go," he said. "Good-bye! Thank you for the pot of gold."

"Good-bye!" said the Fairy Shoemaker. "Much good may the pot of gold do you when you get it." Then—pop! He was gone.

Tom ran home as fast as he could go. He got a spade and ran back to the woods, to dig up the pot of gold. When he got there, what do you think he saw?

Every tree in the woods had a yellow scarf tied around it! The ends of the scarfs waved in the breeze. The bright color made the woods look very gay.

But where was the pot of gold? There were hundreds of trees in the woods. Tom could not dig under the roots of all of them.

Tom was so surprised that the spade fell out of his hands. Then he picked it up, put it over his shoulder, and went home.

The Fairy Shoemaker had beaten him again.

"Mother is right," said Tom. "He is a tricky elf. I shall get a pot of gold sooner if I earn it for myself."

Sarah A. Haste.

119. The First Umbrella

Once an elf-child went out to play. He was an odd little fellow who wore a queer little coat. The bottom of this coat was cut into sharp points.

The elf-child wore a pointed cap and tiny pointed shoes. Even his little ears and nose were pointed.

He was having a good play. He rang the blue-bells and blew the trumpet-flowers. Then he tied a spider's thread to a bit of thistle-down and made a kite.

He ran after his kite until by and by he was far from home. Then the rain began to fall. The big drops came thick and fast.

"This is a new cap and coat," said the elf. "I do not want to get them wet. What shall I do? Oh, I know what to do! I will hide under a big leaf."

So the elf hunted for a leaf big enough to keep him dry. But he could not find one.

Then he saw a toadstool. "Oh, this toadstool is better than a leaf!" he said. "It will keep me snug and dry."

So the elf crept under the toadstool. But someone else was already there. It was a little mouse, fast asleep.

Now the elf was afraid of a mouse.

"If I stay here, this great beast may eat me up," he said. "If I go away my new cap and coat will get wet. What shall I do?"

The elf peeped around the stem of the toadstool. But the mouse had not seen him.

He was still fast asleep.

Then the elf thought of something. He smiled to himself. "I know what to do to keep my coat and cap dry!" he said.

He began to pull at the stem of the toadstool. He put both arms around it, and pulled and pulled. It was very heavy, but at last it came up.

Then the elf-child ran off with the toad- stool over his head.

The mouse was left out in the rain. He got up and shook himself. "Squeak, squeak!" he said. "How very wet I am! Where is that toadstool?"

The toadstool was far away. The elf-child was holding it over his head. He was snug and dry, and his new cap and coat were safe.

"Now I know what to do when it rains!" he said.
And that was the first umbrella.

Carolyn S. Bailey, Adapted.

120. The Twelve Months

I

Laura and Clara were sisters. They had no father or mother, so they lived with an old woman in a little hut near the great forest.

Laura was kind and gentle, but Clara was cross and fretful.

Now, the old woman always let Clara do as she pleased, but she was very unkind to Laura. This was because Clara was like her, for the old woman was cross and fretful, too.

So Laura had to do all the hard work. She had to wait upon Clara and the old woman.

One winter morning Clara was sitting by the fire. It was cold, and she was very cross.

"How I hate winter!" she said. "There is nothing to do but to sit by the fire. I want spring to come. I want some violets. Laura, go out and get some violets!"

"Ask me to do something that can be done," said Laura, laughing. "The violets are all asleep under the snow."

"Why do you laugh?" said the old woman. "Do as your sister tells you."

She opened the door and pushed Laura out. Then she locked the door.

Laura went into the forest. It was very cold, and she had no coat. She went on and on until she came to a great fire.

Twelve old men sat around the fire. Each was wrapped in a great cloak. Three were in cloaks that looked like the leaves of spring. Three were in yellow like the golden grain of summer. Three were in white like the snow of winter. And three wore cloaks like the grapes of autumn.

Each one of the old men held a long wand in his hand.

"Why have you come here?" said one of them to Laura.

"I am looking for violets," said Laura.

"Violets in winter!" cried the old man. "This is no time for violets. Go home and wait for spring."

"Oh, I cannot go home unless I take some violets to my sister!" said Laura. "Can you not help me?"

"This is our work," said the old men in the cloaks like the leaves of spring. They waved their wands over the fire, and the air became soft and warm. The grass grew green, and violets peeped out from it, for spring had come.

Laura picked a great bunch of violets. "Oh, thank you, thank you!" she said to the old men.

As she spoke, the three old men in white waved their wands over the fire, and it was winter again. Snow covered the ground, and a cold wind blew.

Then Laura ran back to the little hut and gave the violets to Clara.

But the violets did not make Clara happy. She did not even put them into water to keep them fresh. She sat by the fire, and tore the pretty flowers to pieces, one by one.

II

The next day Clara was as fretful and cross as ever.

"There is nothing but snow, snow, snow," she said to the old woman. "I wish I had some strawberries. Make Laura get me some ripe, red strawberries."

"Get strawberries in winter!" said Laura. "How can I do that? Come with me. Let us run and jump about in the snow. Then you will learn to like it. You will get warm and rosy."

"Do as your sister tells you, Laura. Get her some strawberries," said the old woman, crossly. She pushed her out and locked the door.

Again Laura went into the forest. Again she found the twelve old men around the great fire.

"Why have you come back?" they said.

"I am looking for strawberries this time," said Laura.

"Strawberries in winter!" cried the old men. "Go home and wait for summer."

"Oh, I cannot go home until I find the berries. I am afraid to go back without them. Please help me," said Laura.

"This is our work," said the men in the golden cloaks. They waved their long wands over the fire.

Then the ice and the snow melted. The air became very warm. Flowers bloomed, and birds sang. Many little plants grew among the thick grass. White flowers covered the plants and turned to bright red berries.

Laura filled her apron with the red berries. "Oh, thank you, thank you!" she said to the old men.

Then the three old men in white waved their wands over the fire. Again snow and ice covered everything. Laura ran home and gave the berries to Clara.

Clara did not even thank her sister, and she was just as cross as ever.

III

The next morning Clara took her old place by the fire. The snow was falling fast. Laura was very busy. She made the beds, washed the dishes, and swept the floor. She sang as she worked.

"I want something," said Clara. "I don't know what I want, but I want something! I hate winter."

"Try to be happy," said Laura. "Let us go out to play in the snow. Let us make snowballs and see how far we can throw them."

"I do not want to make snow-balls," said Clara. "You shall get some bright red apples. Get me a whole apronful of them."

"Go out and get the apples!" said the old woman. "Be quick about it! How can you talk about snow-balls? You know that your sister does not like snow." She pushed her out and locked the door.

So Laura went again to the great fire. When she saw the twelve old men she began to cry.

"How can I ask them for anything more?" she said to herself.

But they were sorry for her. "What is it now, dear child?" they asked.

"I must find some ripe, red apples," said Laura. "I dare not go home without them."

"This is our work," said the old men in cloaks like the grapes of autumn. They waved their wands over the fire. The ice and snow were gone.

Bright leaves were falling from the trees. Nuts were ripe. Laura saw an apple tree covered with rosy fruit.

She shook the tree, and a few apples fell. She shook it again, but no more came down; so she gathered the apples into her apron.

"It is not an apronful," she said, "but I cannot ask for more." She thanked the old men for their kindness to her.

Then she hurried through the forest to the little hut and gave all the apples to her sister.

"You have not brought me an apronful!" said the cross child. "You have been eating them yourself. Where did you get them?"

Laura told her about the old men and the great fire.

"Come with me," said Clara to the old woman. "We will get all the apples on the tree. Laura shall have none of them."

IV

Clara and the old woman dressed themselves warmly and went into the forest.

At last they reached the place where the twelve old men sat around the fire.

"Why have you come here?" asked one of them, just as he had asked Laura.

"That is my business," said Clara. "But if you must know, I came to get some ripe, red apples."

"This is not the season for apples," said the old men. "This is winter."

"How silly you are!" said the old woman. "Tell this poor child where to find apples. You know all about it, because you told her sister. Be quick. Don't keep us waiting in the cold."

The twelve old men looked very angry. Then the three in white cloaks stood up and waved their wands.

The fire went out. The snow fell fast. The wind blew fiercely and shook the trees. The branches snapped and fell.

Clara and the old woman turned to go back, but they were blinded by the thick snow. They could not see the path and they were lost in the forest. They never found their own home again. They wandered far, far away.

Laura was left alone in the little hut.

But the twelve old men never forgot her. For they were the Twelve Months. The three men in white stopped up the cracks in the little hut with snow, so that the cold wind could not get in.

The three men in yellow filled her barn with hay and grain for her horse and cow and chickens.

The three men in cloaks like grapes stored her cellar with apples and potatoes and turnips and beets to last through the long winter.

She was always gentle and kind, and her face was as bright as a day in spring.

Then all the people said, "The Twelve Months love our dear Laura, for when she has winter at the door, she has summer in the barn, autumn in the cellar, and spring in her heart."

Bohemian Tale.

121. The Merman and the Mermaid

Who would be
A merman bold,
Sitting alone,
Singing alone
Under the sea,
With a crown of gold,
On a throne?

Who would be
A mermaid fair,
Singing alone,
Combing her hair
Under the sea,
In a golden curl
With a comb of pearl,
On a throne?

Alfred, Lord Tennyson.

122. The Foolish Goose

Time—One Bright Morning
Place—A Big Road

Persons:

Gray Goose   Wise Old Crow

White Crane   Brownie Hen

A Farmer

[Gray Goose goes walking down the road, with a big bag of corn—very proud and happy. He meets Wise Old Crow.]

Wise Old Crow: Good morning, Gray Goose! What a heavy bag you have there! It is too much for you to carry alone. Let me help you.

Gray Goose: Oh, no! It is a big bag of corn, but I can carry it without any help.

Wise Old Crow: Oh, well, I just wanted to help you as a friend. How long do you think your bag of corn will last you? I can tell you of a plan to make a little corn go a long way.

Gray Goose: What is your plan? Tell me how to make my corn go a long way, Wise Old Crow.

[He puts down his bag of corn in the road.]

Wise Old Crow: First, you must spread your corn out upon the ground, so that we can count it. Then, you count on one side, and I will count on the other side.

[Gray Goose takes some of the corn out of the bag and spreads it upon the ground.]

Gray Goose: [Counting.] One, two, three, four, five, six, seven, eight, nine—

Wise Old Crow: [Eating a grain of corn each time he counts.] One, two, three, four, five, six, seven, eight, nine—

Gray Goose: [Looking up.] What are you doing, Wise Old Crow? Stop eating my corn!

Wise Old Crow: [As he flies far away, laughing.] Caw! Caw! Caw! I told you that I knew a plan to make a little corn go a long way!

[Gray Goose picks up his bag of corn, which is not so heavy now, and goes along the road. After a while he meets White Crane.]

378

White Crane: Good morning, Gray Goose! What have you in your bag?

Gray Goose: Oh, that is some of the best corn in the world.

White Crane: Is that all? You carry it with such care that I thought it must be pearls or diamonds.

Gray Goose: No, I never saw any pearls or diamonds. I should like very much to see such sights!

White Crane: Well, just swim out to that big rock in the lake over there. The bottom of the lake is covered with beautiful pearls and diamonds. I will keep your corn for you.

[Gray Goose swims out to see the wonderful sights. While he is gone White Crane eats nearly all of the corn. Gray Goose cannot see any pearls or diamonds on the bottom of the lake. When he starts back, he sees White Crane eating the corn.]

Gray Goose: Go away from my corn, White Crane! Go away from my corn!

White Crane: [As he flies off, laughing.] I told you that I would keep your corn for you, Gray Goose!

[Gray Goose picks up the little corn that is left, and goes on down the road. After a while he meets Brownie Hen and her ten chicks.]

Brownie Hen: What have you in that little bag, Gray Goose?

Gray Goose: Oh, just a few grains of corn. I had a big bag full, but White Crane ate most of it while I was looking for pearls and diamonds! I like to see strange sights.

Brownie Hen: Well, if you like to see strange sights, throw your corn upon the road and see what happens.

Gray Goose: No, indeed! I know well enough what would happen! Your ten little chicks would eat every grain of it.

Brownie Hen: No, no! Gray Goose. My chicks will not steal your corn. Throw some of it upon the road. If my little ones eat a single grain, I will give you ten white eggs.

Gray Goose: All right! I agree to that.

[He throws down some corn. The chicks run toward it. But before they can eat it, Brownie Hen makes a noise like a hawk. The chicks run away, and Brownie Hen eats the corn.]

Brownie Hen: I told you that my chicks would not eat your corn, Gray Goose!

[Gray Goose goes on till he meets a Farmer.]

Farmer: What is in your bag, Gray Goose?

Gray Goose: [Sadly.] Only a few grains of corn. My bag of corn grows smaller and smaller. I wish I could make it grow bigger and bigger!

Farmer: Why don't you put the corn in the ground? Then it will grow, and you will always have plenty to eat.

Gray Goose: I will do as you say, Farmer.

[He plants it, and the corn begins to grow. For every grain he planted, Gray Goose has hundreds of grains!]

Gray Goose: At last I have found a way to make my bag of corn grow bigger and bigger, instead of smaller and smaller!

Leora Robinson.

123. Jack And The Beanstalk

I

Once upon a time there was a poor woman who lived in a little house with her son Jack.

"Jack," said his mother, one day, "we have no money for bread. You must take our cow to market and sell her."

So Jack started off to market with the cow. On the way he met a man who had some beautiful beans in his hands.

"My boy, where are you going with your cow?" asked the man.

"I am going to market to sell her," said Jack. "What have you in your hands?"

"I have some very wonderful beans," said the man. "I will give them to you if you will give me the cow."

"Very well," said the foolish boy. So he took the beans and ran home.

When his poor mother saw beans instead of money, she began to cry. "You have given away our cow," she said, "and still we have no money for bread!"

Jack felt very sad, but he said, "These beans look so wonderful that I will plant them. Perhaps they will grow and give us plenty of food." So he planted the beans in the garden.

What a strange sight Jack saw in the morning! In the night the beans had grown so high that the stalks were as big as trees and the tops reached far into the clouds!

"I knew those were wonderful beans!" cried the happy boy. "Perhaps I can find some food at the top of the beanstalk. At least I will climb up to see."

II

Up and up Jack climbed until his home was far below. Still he could not see the top of the beanstalk. By and by he felt so tired that he stopped to rest.

Then he thought of his poor, hungry mother, waiting for food. So again he began to climb higher and higher. After a long time Jack reached the top of the wonderful beanstalk. "What a beautiful country this is!" he cried in surprise.

Not far away he saw a great castle. While he was looking at it, a fairy came and stood by his side. She wore a cap of red silk, and in her hand she carried a wand.

"Listen, my boy," said the fairy, "and I will tell you a story. Once upon a time a good King lived in that castle with his Queen and their little son.

"Not far away lived a great giant, who wanted the King's rich treasures. So one night he came to the castle and killed the King, as he lay asleep.

"Now the Queen had taken the little boy to visit her old nurse, who lived far below upon the earth. When she heard that the King had been killed, the Queen was afraid to go back to the castle.

"So she and her son lived with the good old nurse. When the nurse died, the Queen and the boy still stayed in the little house. Jack, your mother is that poor Queen."

"My dear mother! My poor father!" cried Jack in surprise.

"Everything in this castle belonged to your father," said the fairy. "Are you brave enough to try to win back these treasures?"

"I am afraid of nothing," said the boy.

"Then go to the castle," the fairy said, "and get the hen that lays golden eggs, and the harp that talks."

Jack went at once to the castle. When he blew the horn that hung at the gate, the giant's wife opened the door.

"Go away!" said the woman. "Do you not know that a giant lives here? He will kill you if he sees you. Listen! He is coming now! Hide in that little room!"

Just as Jack hid himself, the great giant came into the castle. He was so heavy that the whole place shook as he walked. His voice was like thunder.

"Wife," he cried, "I smell a man in the castle! Where is he? I will kill him!"

"You smell only the meat for your supper," said his wife. "Sit down and eat."

When the giant had finished eating, he cried, "Wife, bring the magic hen!" So she brought the hen and put it upon the table.

"Lay, good hen!" said the giant. At once the hen laid a golden egg.

"Lay again!" called out the giant. The hen laid another golden egg.

"Lay a third time!" said the giant. Again a golden egg lay upon the table.

Then the giant put the three eggs into his pocket and fell fast asleep.

Now Jack had seen the wonderful hen through a hole in the door. "This is the hen that the fairy told me to get!" he thought.

So when the giant fell asleep, Jack quickly ran out of the castle with the hen.

It did not take Jack long to reach the beanstalk and to climb down. How happy his mother was when he showed her the magic hen, which would make them rich!

III

After this, Jack and his mother had all the gold they wanted. But the young boy could not forget the harp which the fairy had told him to take from the giant.

"Mother," he said one day, "I must go back to the castle and get my father's harp."

So again Jack climbed up the great beanstalk, until he came to the land of the fairy. Then he blew upon the castle horn, and the giant's wife opened the door.

Now she did not know that this was the same boy who had run away with the magic hen, for Jack had grown to be very tall in the time that had passed. So she hid him in the little room, just as she had done the first time he came to the castle.

Soon the giant came home. "I smell BOY!" he cried in a voice like thunder.

"You smell only the fat sheep I have cooked for your dinner," said his wife. "Sit down and eat."

After the giant had finished eating, he called out, "Wife, bring me the magic harp!" So the woman brought him a beautiful harp with golden strings.

"Harp," said the giant, "play for me!" At once soft, sweet music filled the castle.

"Play a more joyful tune!" cried the giant. The harp played such a happy tune that the giant laughed with joy. Never had Jack heard such wonderful music.

"Now play a lullaby!" cried the giant. At once the harp played so sweet a lullaby that the giant fell fast asleep.

Then Jack crept quietly out of the room, and took the magic harp in his arms. But as he ran through the castle door, the harp called out, "Master! Master!"

Up sprang the giant with a great shout. He ran after Jack faster than the wind. But as he ran, the giant stumbled over a stone, and fell to the ground. Before he could get upon his feet, Jack quickly climbed down the beanstalk.

"Mother! Mother!" cried the boy, running to his little house. "Give me our old ax!" Then with a few quick strokes he cut the wonderful beanstalk close to its roots. Over it went upon the earth with a loud crash, and Jack was safe.

At that very moment the fairy stood beside him. "My brave boy," she said, "you have done well. From this day on, you and your mother shall live in plenty."

Old English Tale.

124. The Little Tailor

ACT I

Time—One Afternoon, Long, Long Ago

Place—A Room in the Tailor's Shop

Persons:

Master Tailor   Little Tailor

[Little Tailor sits on a table, sewing. Beside him are his great scissors and his thread. The door opens, and Master Tailor comes in.]

Little Tailor: Welcome to you, Master! Have you been to the King's Palace? Did the King's coat fit him?

[Master Tailor shakes his head sadly and throws the King's coat upon the table.]

Master Tailor: The King would not even see me! He would see no one.

Little Tailor: Is the poor King sick?

Master Tailor: No, he is not sick, but he is very sad. He wishes to marry the beautiful Princess. But her father says that the King shall not marry her until he answers three questions.

Little Tailor: Three questions! Upon my scissors and thread! If I were King, I would answer a hundred questions, to marry so beautiful a Princess.

Master Tailor: But he cannot answer them! No one can answer them! So he sits all day with his head in his hands, thinking of the three questions. He would not even look at this fine new coat.

Little Tailor: But what are these three questions? Maybe I can answer them.

Master Tailor: You are a good little tailor, but you had better stick to your scissors and thread. You cannot answer them.

Little Tailor: But please tell me what these questions are, Master Tailor.

Master Tailor: Well, the three questions are:

How many stars are in the sky?

How many hairs on your head lie?

And last of all, how old am I?

[Little Tailor stops sewing. He puts his head in his hands, and thinks for a moment. Then he gets off the table quickly.]

Little Tailor: I must hurry so that I can get to the King's Palace tonight.

[He puts on his long cloak and pointed hat. Then he picks up the King's coat, and hurries toward the door.]

Master Tailor: [Dropping his work in surprise.] Where are you going? Why are you taking the King's coat?

Little Tailor. Oh, I am off to the Palace to tell the King how to answer the three questions.

[He hurries out.]

ACT II

Time—The Evening of the Same Day

Place—The King's Palace

Persons:

The King	Servant
Courtiers	Door-Keeper
Little Tailor	

[The King sits on his throne with his head in his hands. His courtiers stand about the room looking sad. A servant comes in.]

Servant: Dinner is ready in the Great Hall!

King: Go away! Go away! I cannot eat. [Someone knocks at the door crying, "Open! open!"] What is that noise?

Door-Keeper: A foolish tailor boy is outside.

King: Why does he come to the Palace?

Door-Keeper: He says he can tell you how to answer the three questions.

King: Bring the tailor boy in at once.

[The great door is opened, and Little Tailor comes in with the King's coat on his arm.]

King: You say you can answer the three questions? How do you even know what these questions are?

Little Tailor: My Master was here today with this coat. He told me what the questions are. I can answer them.

King: If you can answer them you shall have anything you wish! First, tell me how many stars are in the sky.

Little Tailor: Give me a pen, some ink, a big sheet of white paper, and a table.

[A Courtier brings them in. Little Tailor puts the paper upon the table and makes a great many black dots upon it. Then he holds it up.]

Little Tailor: There, King! Count the dots!

King: [Shaking his head.] I cannot count them! There are so many dots that no one could count them.

Little Tailor: Very well! So it is with the stars in the sky!

King: [In great joy.] Very good! Very good! Just so I will answer the father of the Princess. That is the only true answer! But now tell me how many hairs there are on my head.

Little Tailor: Take off your crown, O King.

[The King takes off his crown. Little Tailor goes up to him, and pulls out one of his hairs.]

Little Tailor: There! You have one hair less than you had when I came here.

King: [Clapping his hands.] Good again! There could not be a better answer! The father of the Princess will not have a word to say. But now, tell me how to answer the last question. What shall I say when the father of the Princess asks me how old he is?

Little Tailor: Oh, that is the very easiest question of all! He is as old as his tongue, and a little older than his teeth.

King: [He shakes Little Tailor by the hand.] You are indeed a wise Little Tailor! I shall marry the Princess tomorrow. Tell me what you wish to have, and I will give it to you.

Little Tailor: I have only one thing to ask of you. Try on this coat, to see if it fits.

King: I do not need to try on the coat. So wise a tailor is sure to make a coat that fits. You shall make all my coats as long as I live.

All the Courtiers: [Shouting together.] Long live the King! Long live Little Tailor!

Jacob and Wilhelm Grimm.

125. The King and the Goose-Herd

I

Long ago, in a land across the sea, there lived a good King who loved books more than anything else in all the world.

One day the King sat down upon a bench in the castle park, to read. He was tired, and the day was hot, so he fell asleep.

After a while the good King woke up. "I will take a long walk," he said to himself, "and see the beautiful lake." He did not think of his book until he had gone far from the park.

"Perhaps I can find someone to send back for it," thought the King, as he looked about him. On a hillside, not far away, he saw a boy tending a flock of geese.

So the King went to the goose-herd and said to him, "My boy, I left a book upon a bench by the gate in the park. I will give you a silver piece if you will get it for me."

The eyes of the boy sparkled as he saw the piece of money. "I would run to the park many times for such a silver piece," he said. "It is more than I get in a month for tending geese. But what will become of my flock while I am gone?"

"The geese will be all right," answered the King. "I will take care of them."

"You!" cried the boy, laughing. "You are too fat and too slow to watch over geese. They would run away from you and get into the meadow by the lake. Do you see that big black gander? He would lead the whole flock away. No! I cannot leave my geese, even for your piece of silver."

"My boy, I can keep people in order," said the King. "Surely I can take care of a few geese for a little while."

"You keep people in order!" the goose-herd cried in surprise. "Oh, you must be the school-master. But you would find that it is much easier to manage boys than geese!"

"That may be so," said the King. "But get me the book, and I will pay for any harm the geese may do while you are gone."

"Well, then, take my whip," answered the gooseherd, "and I will go. Be sure to keep your eyes on the black gander."

So the King took the whip, and the boy started off toward the castle park. All at once he stopped and called back, "Crack the whip, School-Master! Crack the whip!"

The King swung the whip, first to one side and then to the other, but it made no sound.

"You a school-master!" cried the boy, running back to the King. "And yet you cannot crack a whip! Here, let me show you how to do it."

Taking the whip from the King's hand, the gooseherd swung it over his head and made it crack with a loud noise. At once the geese gathered quickly together. Then the boy ran off for the book, as fast as his legs could carry him.

II

Soon the big black gander lifted up his head and looked about him. When he saw that a strange man held the whip, he flapped his wings and gave a shrill cry.

At once all the geese began to run toward
the meadow by the lake. After them ran the King,
shouting as loud as he could, "Stop! Stop! Come back
to the hillside!"

He tried to crack the whip, but no sound came,
and soon the geese were feeding all over the meadow.
The King worked harder and harder, but he could not
drive even one goose back to the hillside.

"The boy was right, after all," he said to himself.
"It is easier to manage thousands of men than one
flock of geese."

After a while the little goose-herd came back
with the book. He looked for his geese, but they were
running over the meadow, eating the long grass.

"There!" said the angry boy, turning to the King.
"I knew how it would be! And I can never drive them
together by myself. Come and help me!"

Without saying a word, the good King gave the
whip to the boy.

"Stand at this corner of the meadow," said the
goose-herd. "Stretch out your arms! Now, move them
up and down. When I give you the word, shout with
all your might at the geese."

Then the boy set out for the end of the field, where
the big black gander was running about and feeding.

"Now, shout!" called out the goose-herd.

The King stretched out his arms, waved them up and down, and shouted with all his might. At the same time the goose-herd cracked his whip, and the whole flock of geese ran out of the meadow.

"Never again shall anyone get my whip away from me!" said the boy. "I would not give it to the King himself."

The King laughed. "You are right," he said, "for the King is as poor a goose-herd as I am. But here is another silver piece to pay for the harm that the geese have done. Do not be angry with me. I never tended geese before. You see, I am the King."

"The King!" cried the boy in surprise. "Well, you are a kind man, anyway, and everyone says that you are a good King. But just the same, you are a very poor goose-herd."

Old Persian Tale.

126. The Rainbow

Two little clouds one summer day
    Went floating through the sky;
They went so fast they bumped their heads,
    And both began to cry.

Old Father Sun looked down and said,
    "Oh, never mind, my dears;
I'll send my little fairy folks
    To dry your falling tears!"

One fairy came in red so fine,
    And one in orange bright;
Then yellow, green, blue, violet
    Were all at once in sight.

They wiped the cloud tears all away.
    And then from out the sky.
Upon a line the sunbeams made.
    They hung their gowns to dry.

Lizzie M. Hadley.

127. How The Days Got Their Names

I never know what day it is
Unless I hear the name;
Today, tomorrow, yesterday
To me seem all the same.

And so I'm glad they named the days,
A long, long time ago.
I'll tell you how it came about,
For every child should know.

In old times, folks had lots of gods;
The greatest was the sun.
Our Sunday got its name from him.
The week had now begun.

The "Moon-day" next was named, to please
The moon-god, so they say.
Its name is Monday now. I guess
That one "o" slipped away.

Our Tuesday's name comes from Tiu
(You spell it T-u-e),
Who was the old-time god of war.
A god to fear was he!

Old Woden was another god,
The god of wisdom bright.
Old Woden's day is Wednesday now;
Be sure you spell it right.

And Thursday gets its name from Thor,
The god of thunder, loud.
The old folks had no "lightning-day"—
They feared the thunder-cloud!

Our Friday comes from Frigedaeg.
That may seem strange, I know.

It got its name from Woden's wife,
A long, long time ago.

Old Saturn was the god of plants.
The friend of girl and boy;
For Saturday was named for him.
The day of children's joy.

Those old-time folks had fifty gods
Almost, it seems to me.
If they had named a day for each,
How long the week would be!

Appendices

Appendix A:
About the Orton-Gillingham Method

In the early decades of the 1900s, physician Samuel Orton and psychologist Anna Gillingham identified the main phonograms used to write the English language as part of their method for helping people with reading disabilities. Elementary educator Romalda Spalding, a student of Dr. Orton, later expanded upon the work of Orton and Gillingham to create the Spalding Method of teaching reading, writing, and spelling.

Many other Orton-Gillingham programs have since been developed which teach reading through spelling. The phonograms—letters or groups of letters which form sounds—represent the forty-five sounds in the English language. Children first learn the phonograms, then they begin spelling. Spelling words are marked according to phonograms and spelling rules. Amazingly, just seventy-five phonograms and thirty spelling rules can be used to explain most English words—98%, in fact. This is an incredible percentage considering that most people believe that English is not a phonetic language.

Why Write Another Orton Phonogram Reading Program?

There are plenty of Orton-Gillingham programs on the market. My main reason for writing yet another one was that I found the others difficult to implement. I am a mother with five children, and whenever it's been time to teach another child to read, I've been either pregnant, had a baby or toddler, or we were moving cross-country.

It shouldn't be surprising that busy mothers often find these programs difficult to implement at first. In the past, some of them have even required the teacher to take a class in order to be able to teach the course. Now, there are more teaching helps available, but they can be expensive.

So the first thing I wanted was something that was pick-up and go. Teaching the phonograms and dictating spelling words is actually very simple and straight forward. The second thing I wanted was a program that focused, quite simply, on the beginning reader, including a list of spelling words that led straight into an inexpensive, easy-to-find set of stories to read. These were the criteria which led to Reading Lessons Through Literature.

Why Teach the Phonograms?

There are those who argue that learning the seventy-five basic phonograms is more than what is necessary to learn to read. Technically, this is true. Children are adaptable, and their flexible little minds often learn things in spite of our teaching mistakes. I'm not arguing that it's the only way to teach reading. I'm arguing that it's the best way to teach reading, for the following reasons:

1. There is a logic to the spelling of the English language, but without learning the basic phonograms and spelling rules, the logic is difficult to see and apply. Learning to read without knowing all of the phonograms is the same as learning to read without knowing the most common sounds of the individual letters, which is to say that while it may be possible, it's far more difficult than it needs to be. With the basic phonograms and thirty spelling rules, the majority of English words can be understood and spelled. Why give children only some of the tools needed for decoding the language? Math would also seem illogical if we were never taught that each number represents a specific quantity.

2. Those who do not teach a complete phonics program which includes all of the basic phonograms often teach some sight words instead. The common list of sight words, called Dolch words because they were compiled by Dr. Dolch in 1948, includes words that can make up 50-70% of a general text. It is commonly—and erroneously—stated that many of these words cannot be sounded out and therefore must be memorized by sight.

There are 220 Dolch words, 220 words that many children are expected to memorize by sight. Why are 75 basic phonograms considered more difficult than 220 sight words?

3. When programs do not teach all the phonograms, they leave a child with no direction on how to decipher new words which have uncommon phonogram sounds.

4. Proponents of teaching a whole language (sight word heavy) reading program often make a disturbing observation. They point out that children will figure out the phonogram sounds through learning the sight words. In other words, instead of being taught, children are expected to figure it out on their own. No wonder we have a literacy problem in this country.

Comparison of O-G and Phonics Programs

The processes used to teach O-G programs and traditional phonics programs look very different, leading parents and teachers to worry that focusing on spelling as O-G does will mean that it will take a child longer to learn how to read. Although the processes are different, they do include some of the same types of activities.

Phonics programs teach a sound and then some words. Reading Lessons Through Literature and other O-G programs do the same while adding the analysis and teaching the spelling rules, which are often pronunciation rules as well. Children doing an O-G program should be reading their spelling words daily. At six, a child might learn 10-20 new words per week and might be reading 50-100 words every day. The reading practice is there, but it looks different than it does in a traditional phonics program.

Phonics programs typically recommend writing the words, too. It's more of a different way of looking at it than a completely different process. Phonics programs say to practice sounding these words and syllables out, then go write them. O-G programs say to write each sound as you hear it, then go read them.

To adults who have been reading since childhood, it can seem like reading and spelling are two different things, but to the child writing down the spelling words, spelling and reading are the same thing.

Appendix B: Prepared Dictation

After finishing all the levels of Reading Lessons Through Literature, you should be comfortable enough with the phonograms and the spelling rules to analyze any word you come across. Many people continue using this methodology to teach advanced spelling to their children.

My preferred method to continue spelling is through prepared dictation. Selections for prepared dictation are included in English Lessons Through Literature, my grammar program. However, you can do prepared dictation with any text you like.

Dictation should not begin until third or fourth grade, depending on the readiness of the child. A child who has finished Reading Lessons Through Literature but who is not yet ready for dictation could analyze words from his copywork a few times a week instead.

In prepared dictation, children type or write a passage after studying it for five to ten minutes. The basic process was described by Charlotte Mason in her book Home Education. We combine the method with analyzing words according to phonograms and spelling rules.

I know that dictation can sound like a huge, time consuming exercise, especially with multiple children. It's not. We do prepared dictation twice a week, on the "off" days from grammar. First, I try to have my boys read through the spelling rules at least once each week, and we make an effort to analyze words that illustrate the different rules. (If they don't appear naturally through the passages we study, then we occasionally spend some time exploring a rule rather than a passage.) Then, each of my boys studies his passage for about ten minutes. He chooses, sometimes with my help, two or three words to analyze. A passage should not have more than three or four unknown words to be studied, though there's nothing wrong with analyzing extra words. He adds these to his Spelling Journal, analyzing each word syllable by syllable.

The Spelling Journal organizes words according to phonogram or spelling rule, and it is a free download on my site. The Spelling Journal can help identify problem spelling areas. Also, having children read through their Spelling Journals occasionally can help reinforce lessons from their previous studies. If you prefer to avoid printing out workbooks, then you could use the Spelling Journal as a template for creating a Spelling Journal in a composition book.

Dictations may be written or typed. My boys type their dictations. The spelling and grammar checks are turned off in our word processing program, and we increase the font size to 20+ points so that I can read over their shoulders. I read the exercises while each boy takes his turn at the keyboard. I stand behind them so that I can make sure they don't make any mistakes. When a mistake is made, we correct immediately. After the dictation, we analyze, or re-analyze, the missed word. Most weeks, there are no missed words from any of my boys.

Beginners can start with just a sentence or two while older children can type or write up to several paragraphs. We use a variety of sources, including Aesop's fables, literature, Bible verses, poetry, and even my children's free reading choices. It is important to avoid passages which contain incorrect grammar, which many modern books do. However, I've found that dictation goes easier when the child is studying a passage he loves.

Appendix C: Sample Schedules

The following pages have sample schedules. The charts show a detailed day to day plan for the first twelve weeks. The lists show an overview of the progression of all three levels.

Level 1: Spelling Lists 1-29

Level 2: Spelling Lists 30-75

Level 3: Spelling Lists 76-127

The first schedules are at the regular pace for starting with younger children, approximately Kindergarten age. This pace will take three years to complete three levels. The schedule begins teaching two phonograms per day and fifteen words per week.

The second schedules are at an accelerated pace for starting with older children, approximately first grade age. This pace will take two years to complete three levels. The schedule begins teaching four phonograms per day and twenty words per week.

Keep in mind, though, that you can and should adjust the pace to make the program work for you. The schedules are only here to give a general idea of how to use the program. Reduce the number of words down to only ten per week for a child who is overwhelmed by fifteen, or dictate only three words every day for a child who is overwhelmed by the writing. Increase the number of words for a child who needs more of a challenge.

The stories are not specifically scheduled. The child may read each story when he's covered the spelling list for the story and he's comfortable reading the words, even if he's still sounding them out. That will vary from child to child.

	Monday	Tuesday	Wednesday	Thursday	Friday
1	Learn c, a	Learn d, g Review Phonograms	Learn o, qu Phonogram Quiz	Learn i, j Review Phonograms	Learn m, n Phonogram Quiz
2	Learn r, l Review Phonograms	Learn h, k Review Phonograms	Learn b, p Phonogram Quiz	Learn t, u Review Phonograms	Learn y, e Phonogram Quiz
3	Learn f, s Review Phonograms	Learn v, w Review Phonograms	Learn x, z Phonogram Quiz	Learn th, ck Review Phonograms	Learn ai, ay Phonogram Quiz
4	Learn sh, ng Review Phonograms List 1-A (5 words)	Learn ee, oo Review Phonograms Read Spelling Words	Learn ou, ow Phonogram Quiz List 1-A (5 words), Read	Learn ar, ch Review Phonograms Read Spelling Words	Learn au, aw Phonogram Quiz List 1-B (5 words), Read
5	Learn oi, oy Review Phonograms List 1-B (5 words), Read	Learn er, ur Review Phonograms Read Spelling Words	Learn ir, ear Phonogram Quiz List 1-C (5 words), Read	Learn wor, wh Review Phonograms Read Spelling Words	Learn ea, or Phonogram Quiz List 1-C (5 words), Read
6	Learn ed, ew Review Phonograms List 1-D (5 words), Read	Learn cei, gu Review Phonograms Read Spelling Words	Learn wr, augh Phonogram Quiz List 1-D (5 words), Read	Learn ui, oa Review Phonograms Read Spelling Words	Learn ph, oe Phonogram Quiz List 1-E (5 words), Read

	Monday	Tuesday	Wednesday	Thursday	Friday
7	Learn tch, dge Review Phonograms List 1-E (5 words), Read	Learn ey, bu Review Phonograms Read Spelling Words	Learn ei, eigh Phonogram Quiz List 1-F (5 words), Read	Learn ci, ti Review Phonograms Read Spelling Words	Learn si, kn Phonogram Quiz List 1-F (5 words), Read
8	Learn igh, ie Review Phonograms List 1-G (5 words), Read	Learn gn, ough, mb Review Phonograms	Phonogram Quiz Read Spelling Words List 1-G (5 words)	Review Phonograms Read Spelling Words	Phonogram Quiz Read Spelling Words List 1-H (5 words)
9	Review Phonograms Read Spelling Words List 1-H (5 words)	Review Phonograms Read Spelling Words	Phonogram Quiz Read Spelling Words List 1-I (5 words)	Review Phonograms Read Spelling Words	Phonogram Quiz Read Spelling Words List 1-I (5 words)
10	Review Phonograms Read Spelling Words List 1-J (5 words)	Review Phonograms Read Spelling Words	Phonogram Quiz Read Spelling Words List 1-J (5 words)	Review Phonograms Read Spelling Words	Phonogram Quiz Read Spelling Words List 1-K (5 words)
11	Review Phonograms Read Spelling Words List 1-K (5 words)	Review Phonograms Read Spelling Words	Phonogram Quiz Read Spelling Words List 1-L (5 words)	Review Phonograms Read Spelling Words	Phonogram Quiz Read Spelling Words List 1-L (5 words)
12	Review Phonograms Read Spelling Words List 1-M (5 words)	Review Phonograms Read Spelling Words	Phonogram Quiz Read Spelling Words List 1-M (5 words)	Review Phonograms Read Spelling Words	Phonogram Quiz Read Spelling Words List 1-N (5 words)

Year 1

Week 1 Phonograms c through n

Week 2 Phonograms r through e

Week 3 Phonograms f through ay

Week 4 Phonograms sh through aw

             Spelling Lists: 1-A, half 1-B

Week 5 Phonograms oi through or

             Spelling Lists: half 1-B, 1-C

Week 6 Phonograms ed through oe

             Spelling Lists: 1-D, half 1-E

Week 7 Phonograms tch through kn

             Spelling Lists: half 1-E, 1-F

Week 8 Phonograms igh through mb

             Spelling Lists: 1-G, half 1-H

Week 9 Spelling Lists: half 1-H, 1-I

Week 10 Spelling Lists: 1-J, half 1-K

Week 11 Spelling Lists: half 1-K, 1-L

Week 12 Spelling Lists: 1-M, half 1-N

Week 13 Spelling Lists: half 1-N, 1-O

Week 14 Spelling Lists: 1-P, half 1-Q

Week 15 Spelling Lists: half 1-Q, 1-R

Week 16 Spelling Lists: 1-S, half 1-T

Week 17 Spelling Lists: half 1-T, 2

Week 18 Spelling Lists: 3, half 4

Week 19 Spelling Lists: half 4, 5

Week 20 Spelling Lists: 6, half 7

Week 21 Spelling Lists: half 7, 8

Week 22 Spelling Lists: 9, half 10

Week 23 Spelling Lists: half 10, 11

Week 24 Spelling Lists: 12, half 13

Week 25 Spelling Lists: half 13, 14

Week 26 Spelling Lists: 15, half 16

Week 27 Spelling Lists: half 16, 17

Week 28 Spelling Lists: 18, half 19

Week 29 Spelling Lists: half 19, 20

Week 30 Spelling Lists: 21, half 22

Week 31 Spelling Lists: half 22, 23

Week 32 Spelling Lists: 24, half 25

Week 33 Spelling Lists: half 25, 26

Week 34 Spelling Lists: 27, half 28

Week 35 Spelling Lists: half 28, 29

Year 2

Week 1 Phonograms c through e

Week 2 Phonograms f through aw

Week 3 Phonograms oi through oe

Week 4 Phonograms tch through mb

        Spelling List: 2

Week 5 Spelling Lists: 3-4

Week 6 Spelling Lists: 5-6

Week 7 Spelling Lists: 7-8

Week 8 Spelling Lists: 9-10

Week 9 Spelling Lists: 11-12

Week 10 Spelling Lists: 13-14

Week 11 Spelling Lists: 15-16

Week 12 Spelling Lists: 17-18

Week 13 Spelling Lists: 19-20

Week 14 Spelling Lists: 21-22

Week 15 Spelling Lists: 23-24

Week 16 Spelling Lists: 25-26

Week 17 Spelling Lists: 27-28

Week 18 Spelling Lists: 29-30

Week 19 Spelling Lists: 31-32

Week 20 Spelling Lists: 33-34

Week 21 Spelling Lists: 35-36

Week 22 Spelling Lists: 37-38

Week 23 Spelling Lists: 39-40

Week 24 Spelling Lists: 41-42

Week 25 Spelling Lists: 43-44

Week 26 Spelling Lists: 45-46

Week 27 Spelling Lists: 47-48

Week 28 Spelling Lists: 49-50

Week 22 Spelling Lists: 51-52

Week 29 Spelling Lists: 53-54

Week 30 Spelling Lists: 55-56

Week 31 Spelling Lists: 57-58

Week 32 Spelling Lists: 59-60

Week 33 Spelling Lists: 61-62

Week 34 Spelling Lists: 63-64

Week 35 Spelling Lists: 65-66

Week 36 Spelling Lists: 67-68

Year 3

Week 1   Phonograms c through e

Week 2   Phonograms f through aw

Week 3   Phonograms oi through oe

Week 4   Phonograms tch through mb

        Spelling Lists: 69-70

Week 5   Spelling Lists: 71-72

Week 6   Spelling Lists: 73-74

Week 7   Spelling Lists: 75-76

Week 8   Spelling Lists: 77-78

Week 9   Spelling Lists: 79-80

Week 10 Spelling Lists: 81-82

Week 11 Spelling Lists: 83-84

Week 12 Spelling Lists: 85-86

Week 13 Spelling Lists: 87-88

Week 14 Spelling Lists: 89-90

Week 15 Spelling Lists: 91-92

Week 16 Spelling Lists: 93-94

Week 17 Spelling Lists: 95-96

Week 18 Spelling Lists: 97-98

Week 19 Spelling Lists: 99-100

Week 20 Spelling Lists: 101-102

Week 21 Spelling Lists: 103-104

Week 22 Spelling Lists: 105-106

Week 23 Spelling Lists: 107-108

Week 24 Spelling Lists: 109-110

Week 25 Spelling Lists: 111-112

Week 26 Spelling Lists: 113-114

Week 27 Spelling Lists: 115-116

Week 28 Spelling Lists: 117-118

Week 29 Spelling Lists: 119-120

Week 30 Spelling Lists: 121-122

Week 31 Spelling Lists: 123-124

Week 32 Spelling Lists: 125-126

Week 33 Spelling Lists: 127

Accelerated Pace for Older Students

	Monday	Tuesday	Wednesday	Thursday	Friday
1	Learn c, a, d, g Review Phonograms	Learn o, qu, i, j Review Phonograms	Learn m, n, r, l Phonogram Quiz	Learn h, k, b, p Review Phonograms	Learn t, u, y, e Phonogram Quiz
2	Learn f, s, v, w Review Phonograms	Learn x, z, th, ck Review Phonograms	Learn ai, ay, sh, ng Phonogram Quiz	Learn ee, oo, ou, ow Review Phonograms	Learn ar, ch, au, aw Phonogram Quiz
3	Learn oi, oy, er, ur Review Phonograms	Learn ir, ear, wor, wh Review Phonograms	Learn ea, or, ed, ew Phonogram Quiz	Learn cei, gu, wr, augh Review Phonograms	Learn ui, oa, ph, oe Phonogram Quiz
4	Learn tch, dge, ey, bu Review Phonograms	Learn ei, eigh, ci, ti Review Phonograms List 1-A	Learn si, kn, igh, ie Phonogram Quiz Read Spelling Words	Learn gn, ough, mb Review Phonograms List 1-B	Phonogram Quiz Read Spelling Words
5	Review Phonograms Read Spelling Words	Review Phonograms List 1-C	Phonogram Quiz Read Spelling Words	Review Phonograms List 1-D	Phonogram Quiz Read Spelling Words
6	Review Phonograms Read Spelling Words	Review Phonograms List 1-E	Phonogram Quiz Read Spelling Words	Review Phonograms List 1-F	Phonogram Quiz Read Spelling Words

	Monday	Tuesday	Wednesday	Thursday	Friday
7	Review Phonograms Read Spelling Words	Review Phonograms List 1-G	Phonogram Quiz Read Spelling Words Phonogram Quiz	Review Phonograms List 1-H Review Phonograms	Phonogram Quiz Read Spelling Words Phonogram Quiz
8	Review Phonograms Read Spelling Words	Review Phonograms List 1-I	Read Spelling Words	Read Spelling Words List 1-J	Read Spelling Words
9	Review Phonograms Read Spelling Words	Review Phonograms Read Spelling Words List 1-K	Phonogram Quiz Read Spelling Words	Review Phonograms Read Spelling Words List 1-L	Phonogram Quiz Read Spelling Words
10	Review Phonograms Read Spelling Words	Review Phonograms Read Spelling Words List 1-M	Phonogram Quiz Read Spelling Words	Review Phonograms Read Spelling Words List 1-N	Phonogram Quiz Read Spelling Words
11	Review Phonograms Read Spelling Words	Review Phonograms Read Spelling Words List 1-O	Phonogram Quiz Read Spelling Words	Review Phonograms Read Spelling Words List 1-P	Phonogram Quiz Read Spelling Words
12	Review Phonograms Read Spelling Words	Review Phonograms Read Spelling Words List 1-Q	Phonogram Quiz Read Spelling Words	Review Phonograms Read Spelling Words List 1-R	Phonogram Quiz Read Spelling Words

Year 1

Week 1   Phonograms c through e

Week 2   Phonograms f through aw

Week 3   Phonograms oi through oe

Week 4   Phonograms tch through mb

    Spelling Lists: 1-A, 1-B

Week 5   Capitals c through e

    Spelling Lists: 1-C, 1-D

Week 6   Capitals f through z

    Spelling Lists: 1-E, 1-F

Week 7   Spelling Lists: 1-G, 1-H

Week 8   Spelling Lists: 1-I, 1-J

Week 9   Spelling Lists: 1-K, 1-L

Week 10 Spelling Lists: 1-M, 1-N

Week 11 Spelling Lists: 1-O, 1-P

Week 12 Spelling Lists: 1-Q, 1-R

Week 13 Spelling Lists: 1-S, 1-T

Week 14 Spelling Lists: 2-3

Week 15 Spelling Lists: 4-5

Week 16 Spelling Lists: 6-7

Week 17 Spelling Lists: 8-9

Week 18 Spelling Lists: 10-11

Week 19 Spelling Lists: 12-13

Week 20 Spelling Lists: 14-15

Week 21 Spelling Lists: 16-17

Week 22 Spelling Lists: 18-19

Week 23 Spelling Lists: 20-21

Week 24 Spelling Lists: 22-23

Week 25 Spelling Lists: 24-25

Week 26 Spelling Lists: 26-27

Week 27 Spelling Lists: 28-29

Week 28 Spelling Lists: 30-31

Week 29 Spelling Lists: 32-33

Week 30 Spelling Lists: 34-35

Week 31 Spelling Lists: 36-37

Week 32 Spelling Lists: 38-39

Week 33 Spelling Lists: 40-41

Week 34 Spelling Lists: 42-43

Week 35 Spelling Lists: 44-45

Week 36 Spelling Lists: 46-47

Year 2

Appendix D: Glossary of Spelling Words

This list of spelling words is in alphabetical order and shows in which lesson each word is analyzed. Lists 1-29 are in Level 1, lists 30-75 are in Level 2, lists 76-127 are in Level 3, and lists 128-173 are in Level 4.

Spelling Words in Alphabetical Order

Spelling Words in Alphabetical Order

Spelling Words in Alphabetical Order

Spelling Words in Alphabetical Order

Made in the USA
Middletown, DE
12 September 2021